# The Challenge of English in the National Curriculum

The introduction of a national curriculum for English has been problematic. While there may be fairly widespread agreement about the principle of establishing a written curriculum for English, the nature of this document has caused much controversy, with many people sharing the belief that such a curriculum must be constantly evolving to meet the particular needs of different schools and teachers.

This book considers how particular aspects of a national curriculum can be reconciled with the best practice of the English teaching tradition. It has been written by teachers working within the present context, but who look at the lessons of the past as well as hopes for the future. The chapter topics originate from questions raised by teachers at in-service workshops as the issues which concern them most, and cover the majority of significant aspects of English within the new revised National Curriculum. They tackle issues in speaking and listening, reading, pre-twentieth century literature, writing, assessment, grammar, the use of IT, and drama and media. Contributions range from John Johnson's survey of practical ways to raise the standard of oracy to Nick Peim's suggestions for coping with Key Stage 4, which leads him to a radical questioning of the whole nature of English as a curriculum subject.

**Robert Protherough** is a freelance lecturer and writer and was formerly Senior Lecturer in Education at Hull University. **Peter King** is Senior Lecturer in Education and PGCE Director at Loughborough University.

D0182804

# The Challenge of English in the National Curriculum

Edited by Robert Protherough and Peter King

London and New York

First published 1995
by Routledge
11 New Fetter Lane, London EC4P 4EE

Simultaneously published in the USA and Canada
by Routledge
29 West 35th Street, New York, NY 10001

© 1995 Selection and editorial matter, Robert Protherough and Peter King;
individual contributions © 1995 the authors

Typeset in Palatino by LaserScript, Mitcham, Surrey
Printed and bound in Great Britain by
TJ Press (Padstow) Ltd, Padstow, Cornwall

*British Library Cataloguing in Publication Data*
A catalogue record for this book is available from the British Library

*Library of Congress Cataloguing in Publication Data*
A catalogue record for this book has been requested

ISBN 0–415–09061–X

# Contents

# Contributors

| | |
|---|---|
| **Chris Abbott** | Senior Research Fellow, Centre for Educational Studies, King's College, University of London |
| **Judith Atkinson** | former Head of English, Wolfreton School, Hull |
| **Peter Brown** | Head of English Faculty, Newland School for Girls, Hull |
| **Paul Evans** | English teacher, Andrew Marvell School, Hull |
| **John Haddon** | Head of English, Littleover Community School, Derby |
| **John Johnson** | Head teacher, The Campion School, Hornchurch, Essex, and NATE Research Officer |
| **Peter King** | Senior Lecturer in Education, Loughborough University |
| **Jane Lodge** | English teacher, Withernsea High School, Humberside |
| **Nick McGuinn** | Lecturer in Education, University of Hull |
| **Nick Peim** | Beauchamp College, Leicester |
| **Robert Protherough** | Author, formerly Senior Lecturer in Education, University of Hull |
| **Jan Sargeant** | Senior teacher/Head of English, Withernsea High School, Humberside |

# Chapter 1

# Introduction

## Whose curriculum?

*Robert Protherough and Peter King*

**WHOSE CURRICULUM AND WHOSE ENGLISH?**

A fairy story. Once upon a time in the Land of Ing the people all did things in their own way, and they argued all the time about which way was best. The Good Fairy got so tired of all their squabbles that she waved her wand and up popped a Magic Curriculum. 'That's the way to do it', said the Good Fairy. 'Hurrah!' shouted the people. So then they all did things the way the Magic Curriculum said, and they all lived happily ever after. The end.

Well, it *was* a fairy story, wasn't it? The imposing style in which a 'national' curriculum was launched may have led some teachers to expect an authoritative and almost permanent statement of principles and practice that all teachers could happily follow. If so, then recent events have shown how misguided they were. It is now impossible to talk of *the* National Curriculum as something definitive. Within five years, four irreconcilable versions of *a* National Curriculum for English have been promulgated (together with an additional variant for Wales) and five committees or working parties have been charged with drafting or revising these documents without ever reaching consensus. The 'revised' Order of 1993 was far more than a revision of Cox's; it was actually grounded in a quite different philosophy from his and embodied different views of what talking, reading and writing actually mean. It is plain, therefore, that even if there may be general agreement about the principle of establishing a written curriculum for English, such a text will have to be tentative, continually changing and evolving, and will have to be adapted to meet the particular needs of different schools and teachers. Those of us who have prepared policy documents and schemes of work (even, in the old days, 'syllabuses') for English departments know that they were always out of date by the time an agreed version was written down, that they were constantly needing to be revised. If we waited until the work on the National Curriculum was 'complete', then we would wait for ever.

As is argued in chapter 3, we cannot now read any document like *English in the National Curriculum* (DES/WO, 1990) as an innocent set of pedagogic guidelines. There are three main reasons for this. First, notions of 'English' and of language have been given a heavy ideological weight. Conflicting social, economic and political forces all make claims on what should count as literacy and how it is to be acquired, and have increasingly dictated the terms in which that debate is carried on. As a subject English has provided the clearest site on which opposing views within the education debate of the last decade could draw up their battle lines. It was the political débâcle over imposed testing arrangements for English in late spring 1993 that brought in support from unions, head teachers, parents and many outsiders concerned for education. The revolt soon became unstoppable and led first to a national boycott of the tests and ultimately to the setting up of the Dearing Review of the National Curriculum and its assessment as a face-saving device for the embattled Secretary of State for Education.

Second, attempts to define and to control what goes on in English have increasingly plainly been seen as attacks on teachers' professionalism. Because English lessons consist of talking, reading and writing, then any attempt to legislate for these activities has a more profound effect on what teachers actually do in the classroom than curriculum proposals do in any other subject area. It has to be understood that the protests of English teachers have been less about the obvious overloading of their time than about the sustained governmental assault on their professionalism, the denigrating of experience and research evidence.

Third, proposals for the curriculum now have to be seen as statements about the resourcing of education. Teachers have detected a shift in balance away from the English classroom, not only in direct governmental intervention, but also in the indirect pressures on school cultures: the greater power of school management, the control of budgets and of in-service provision, the perceived need to 'compete' – all tending to define objectives, policy, resourcing from outside the English department, and thus reducing still further the autonomy of teachers. The unsteady structure of attainment targets, league tables, teacher appraisal, 'parental choice' of opted-out schools, links teaching and the curriculum to the funding of schools and the salaries of teachers.

From the English teacher's viewpoint, therefore, these years of attempting to understand and implement an ever-shifting curriculum and assessment system have been years of chaos, frustration and anger. Much of that frustration has been caused by trying to argue educational principles against individuals and bodies who are working solely to a political agenda. For example, there were the serious disagreements with SEAC and the DfE over the principles on which the testing system was built. Teachers argued that the national tests were ill-conceived with no proven evidence of their reliability or validity, but they were confronting a political agenda of forcing simplistic accountability on schools through national league tables. Their concern at being increasingly reduced to operatives who delivered someone else's curriculum was brought into sharp focus by the NCC Review, instigated by the Secretary of State in late 1992. Many teachers objected to the way in which political pressure groups were being encouraged in their attempts to hijack the curriculum in ways which denied the practical good sense of teachers and which pushed aside the principles on which the original Cox committee's report had sought to establish agreement ('enabling rather than restricting', 'starting point not a straitjacket'). The members of the review team, experienced in teaching English, were not free agents; they were overseen by a Review Group 'which guided the detailed work from a policy perspective'. Although other teachers were 'consulted' by the NCC, it is no secret that any advice they gave that conflicted with the official stance was ignored and not even reported. Similarly, in the Dearing Review process the advice of the English working group on some points was simply overruled by the SCAA committee. Political and administrative considerations have been allowed to dominate educational and professional ones.

The experiences of recent years have therefore made teachers healthily sceptical about centralised policies for English, and they find themselves oddly aligned with the one-time DES spokesman Michael Fallon, who says that 'a prescriptive curriculum is a nonsense in a free society'. Even more oddly, they find that Sheila Lawlor pins the blame for the National Curriculum not on the government but on them. It is, she writes, 'the organ for enforcing an educational consensus on all' and has been 'systematically imposed on the content and method of teaching by the regiments of the education "service": teacher trainers, inspectors, education officials and theorists, exam boards and teachers' (*The Observer*, 20 February 1994). It is a strange contortion of events to see teachers imposing a prescriptive curriculum on the country rather than the other way round!

This introduction was written at a time when the Dearing Review put on temporary hold the process of ceaseless change, and therefore offered a suitable time to consider what a curriculum for English might be like.

The sections that follow suggest why English has traditionally been a focus for controversy, place current disputes in a wider context, consider how the curricular debate has posed a threat to professionalism, and finally look ahead to encourage English teachers to reassert the values in which they believe.

## WHY ENGLISH IS CONTROVERSIAL

There are good reasons that controversy has particularly centred on the form and place of English in the National Curriculum and that the 1993 boycott of testing was largely driven by objections to the form of the English tests.

The reasons are inherent in the nature of the subject and its teaching, and five significant points can be briefly outlined.

- First, English is contentious because of the importance generally attached to the subject and related concepts of 'Englishness'. This is not simply because it is seen as 'central' and 'indispensable' in the curriculum, 'the only basis possible for a national education' (as the Newbolt Report put it in 1921), affecting the learning that goes on in all areas and offering essential preparation for adult working life. Arguments about how children should speak and write, what they should read, or what knowledge of language they should have, are really arguments about how education should shape young people's views of the world. Controlling English is seen as one way of controlling society. Professor Cox has rightly said that 'a National Curriculum in English is intimately involved with questions about our national identity, indeed with the whole future ethos of British society. The teaching of English . . . affects the individual and social identity of us all' (Cox, 1990, p. 2). Some groups who share this belief wish to impose a curriculum or methodology that will force particular values down the throats of students or their teachers (as is illustrated in chapter 4 among others). Such a wish is blind to the fact that English resists being used in such a doctrinaire way, because the shared language that we all speak is essentially uncontrollable, as are our reactions to what we read. 'The work of English teaching involves continual pressing for the expression of alternative ideas, inviting challenge to received opinions, seeking strong personal responses, establishing debate' (Protherough and Atkinson, 1991, p. 15).
- Second, what we conventionally call 'English' is controversial because of the continuing debate about just what the subject really is (this is taken further in chapter 11). Many studies have pointed to its 'unique' or 'special' nature, and it is particularly difficult to tie down neatly on paper a subject where there is no real consensus about its content and boundaries. In recent years, direct and indirect pressures have brought about changes in the definition of the subject, its principles and practice, and the shape of its curriculum. Most immediately, English has been reshaped by developments within the profession. These have included teachers' reactions to educational development and research and the dissemination of new classroom approaches through professional organisations like NATE. Teachers have reacted in different ways to the widening of such concepts as 'text' or 'literature' and to the shifting boundaries between their subject and Drama and Media (or

Cultural) Studies (a topic addressed in chapter 10 of this volume). The Cox Report pointed out that there are at least five distinct models of 'English', each with its own particular emphasis, that currently animate the work of different teachers. There are particular difficulties in balancing the different contributions that English is expected to make to so many 'areas of experience' in the curriculum. English draws its theoretical support from a whole range of disciplines, the social sciences and sciences like linguistics as well as humanities and the arts; it is concerned with the personal and subjective as well as the objective. It is therefore particularly hard to fit such a subject into any generalised view of the curriculum that treats all subjects as alike, as though all can equally be defined in terms of behavioural objectives, ten-level sequential development and skills that can be neatly defined and tested.

- Third, English is contentious because of its particular openness and responsiveness to influences from society and its shifting educational goals. Policies for English have to be framed and evolve in changing local, national and global contexts. Shifting views of the function of education in general (the relative importance attached to preparation for work in a competitive economy, socialisation within a cultural heritage, or personal development and pleasure in learning) significantly affect the way that English is realised. It is a subject about which expectations are rightly high, and allegations of falling 'standards' in reading or inaccurate spelling can always make headlines in the popular press. In part this is because English is a subject about which everybody feels entitled to have an opinion, from the heir to the throne downwards, unlike Physics or German, say. So it is that, for example, in recent years English teachers have responded to the pressures from different groups to frame a curriculum more concerned for the rights and needs of ethnic minorities, to reshape conventional assumptions about gender, to offer the higher levels of functional literacy thought to be required in industrial societies, and to prepare students to exploit information technology (see chapter 9). Simultaneously, and overlapping these direct pressures for change in subject English, it has been influenced by the growing sense of world crisis, the communications explosion and wider social developments. English teachers, like others, feel themselves faced by greater questioning of their professionalism, demands for accountability in times of recession, more vocal concern for parental rights, the vision of education as a lifelong process. English lessons are increasingly grappling with broader issues like concern for the environment, nationalist conflicts, social mobility and unemployment, or the problems of juvenile crime. Any national policy for English has to be framed within the context of a particular society, culture and time, and must model those choices that may be possible within the material constraints of factors like budgets, buildings, teacher supply, and student enrolment. It is manifestly difficult to create a coherent English policy within a culture that is itself socially divided, that lacks common values and that has no shared view of educational goals.

- Fourth, English is controversial because it calls into question conventional methods and criteria of assessment. It was no accident that English teachers were among the first and the strongest proponents of coursework assessment and were sceptical of the value of narrow skills-based testing. An English programme has many possible criteria for success, and it is extremely difficult to decide how far any of them have been met. If the aim is to produce individuals who are sensitive, articulate, responsive, imaginative, reflective language users, then when are they believed to have reached that point? When can the programme be said to have 'succeeded'? Teachers of language are by training equipped to be sceptical of those perennial slogans ('restoring the basic skills') consisting of resonant emotional metaphors that can be adapted to a range of meanings. Nobody can be against 'raising standards' or removing 'inequalities' in the name of 'social justice' or pressing for 'excellence'. All depends on the measures that are proposed to achieve these laudable aims. How precisely are their effects to be assessed? Attempts at monitoring can lead to an overemphasis on those goals that can be measured and those results or skills that can be tested as is argued in chapter 6.
- Fifth, English is controversial because of the distinct way in which its teachers see themselves and their work. This is not simply because by training they are likely to be articulate and prepared to look critically at proposals that affect them. From the time of the Newbolt Report onwards, English teachers have traditionally had a 'high' view of their role as concerned with changing lives rather than simply imparting knowledge. Effective English teachers see themselves as 'different' from teachers of other subjects, marked by a distinct personal relationship with their subject and their students. In a recent survey, over half believed that they worked in the classroom in ways that marked them off from others. In considering potential entrants to the profession 80 per cent of them saw qualities of personality and attitude as the dominant qualifications. It is also significant that the most important influence on their development as teachers was seen as other English teachers (rather than their studies, advisers or professional tutors) which – together with a high ranking for professional associations – suggests the importance they attached to a co-operative learning community and a sense of group solidarity (Protherough and Atkinson, 1991, chapters 1 and 2). As will be suggested in following sections, the evolution of an English curriculum and its associated methodology had until recently taken place within that community.

The enquiry cited in Protherough and Atkinson (1991) found that the successful teachers surveyed, although very different in background and educational experience, described changes in their own practice in very similar terms that embodied the implicit values of that particular cultural group. Although they were well aware of the need for English programmes to have what they called 'structure', 'coherence' and 'sequence', what they valued for themselves was the 'freedom', 'variety', 'range' and 'diversity' available to English teachers. It is not surprising, then, that when asked what the most urgent problems were that faced English teachers, the most frequent response was to mention the coming of the National Curriculum, seen in terms of 'imposed' models and 'interference' with teachers' autonomy (Protherough and Atkinson, 1991, chapter 9).

## THE CONTEXT OF POLICY FRAMING IN ENGLISH

The short history of English as a subject is largely the story of successive attempts at particular moments to give some form to an ever-changing stream of ideas about how the subject is to be learned and taught. Such policies, of which models for the curriculum form a part, always look in two directions: diagnosing on the basis of the past and prescribing for an uncertain future. For implementation they depend on a degree of accord between policy-makers, administrators, teachers and society as a whole (and, of course, policies for English are ultimately inseparable from policies for other subjects and for education generally).

The continuing consultations and reviews of the curriculum have always posed a number of questions. First, what is to be the balance between centralised and regional or local decision-making? There has always been a 'triangle of tension' between central government, local administration and individual schools and colleges. Second, whose voices should be heard in framing a policy and which should be dominant? Third, what is the relationship between the formulation of policy and its actual implementation, and how will that be monitored? Fourth, what is to be the balance between professional approaches to the framing of policy, concentrating on input (the style and quality of teaching; the motivation, skills and training of English teachers) and the bureaucratic, emphasising output (assessing the efficiency of the system by testing, norm-referencing and benchmarks)? Our argument is that the answers given to these questions since the 1980s have been radically different from those offered at any earlier time, and that this change underlies the present discontent.

Over eighty years ago, the Board of Education's first major official report on *The Teaching of English in Secondary Schools* (Board of Education, 1910) admirably established a tradition for defining the principles of a curricular policy for English. Among the forward-looking suggestions were the (then revolutionary) ideas that literature and composition are 'organically interrelated', that children should be encouraged to talk to one another in class, that English should be studied as a living language without too much attention to grammar, that Literature must be based on 'first hand study', that Shakespeare's plays should be read through rapidly and practically without comment, that surface errors in writing are less important than failings of style and structure, that revision of writing should be encouraged, and that teachers must not allow themselves to be dominated by the supposed requirements of external examinations.

At the same time, the third paragraph made a significant disclaimer, in saying that the report:

> does not profess to frame a syllabus of instruction or to prescribe in detail the methods by which teachers should proceed. Any such attempt would be useless, if not actually harmful, for several reasons. In the first place, English is the last subject in which a teacher should be bound by hard and fast rules. No subject gives more scope for individuality of treatment or for varied experiment; in none is the personal quality of the teacher more important. In the second place, schools themselves differ materially from one another [and] these differences must be met by corresponding varieties of method. . . . *In this diversity of conditions, no external authority can or ought to offer detailed guidance. General principles must be translated into practice by the teacher.* [Our italics]

A tacit convention was thus established between teachers on one side and those on the other side with statutory duties to ensure effective schooling, nationally or regionally, that there would be continuing discussion and consultation about principles, but that for a variety of reasons there would be no central prescription of curriculum or methodology. For many years, the education ministers of different parties generally acted in an 'arm's-length' way upon professional advice, essentially rubber-stamping the decisions put forward by the DES and HMI. The post-war years of educational expansions were repeatedly described as a time of partnership and consensus. It was ironical that the partnership ended in the 1980s just at the time when increased public expectations of the system should have strengthened it. The failure to achieve professional consensus about policy within English teaching was accompanied by a wider failure to convince those outside the profession, that thus opened the way for more direct political intervention. This is generally dated from the speech of James Callaghan at Ruskin College, Oxford, in October 1976, initiating the so-called 'great debate' over education policy.

A string of policy papers from the Department of Education and Science, Her Majesty's Inspectors and subject associations centred on the future form of the curriculum. The repeated theme was the need for a curriculum that would be broad, balanced and coherent, and that would provide greater continuity across the different phases of education to the age of 16. Among the different subject papers published by HMI, *English for Ages 5 to 16* (DES, 1984) was unique in producing such massive and vigorous reactions that it had to be followed swiftly by another entitled *English for Ages 5 to 16: The Responses* (DES, 1986). The original document defined the aims of English teaching in terms of 'achieving competence in the many and varied uses of our language', briefly applied this to speech, reading and writing, and added 'a fourth aim which applies over all the modes of language . . . to teach pupils *about* language'. The bulk of the pamphlet was given over to defining objectives that pupils of 7, 11 and 16 'should' know or be able to do (sixty of them at age 16), and detailing some principles of assessment that occupied about a third of the whole. The many critics attacked the functional emphasis, especially in 'knowledge about language', and the comparative disregard for literary studies, for media studies or for cultural diversity. The proposed statements of essentially behavioural objectives, according to the *Responses* paper, 'evoked widespread disfavour especially from the profession', and there was 'clear professional dissent from the notion of periodic testing'. The debate brought into the open the wide divisions in society over the formulation of policies for English. Whereas only a quarter of the responses from schools and colleges broadly approved of the report, three-quarters of the letters from the public were unreserved in their approval of it. Kenneth Baker and others were to cite such instances in order to claim that there was public concern over the teaching of English and that the subject was too important to be left to the professionals.

## THE POLITICISING OF ENGLISH TEACHING

In the 1980s Sir Keith Joseph started to use the powers formally vested in him as Secretary of State to curtail discussion with professional groups and to formulate policy directly through legislation. Although he said that the Curriculum Matters series was intended to initiate a 'consultative process', he made plain in his introduction to the English volume that 'the development of agreed national objectives for English teaching is . . . a particularly important part of the Government's policies for raising standards in schools'. It was his successor as Secretary of State for Education, Kenneth Baker, who eventually used the powers of his office to make those 'agreed national objectives' mandatory, within the framework of the 1988 Education Act. In keeping with the market ideology of the government, that Act claimed to be devolving power from the 'producers' (teachers, local authorities, advisers and what were called disparagingly 'educationalists') towards the 'customers' (assumed without debate to be the parents of school children). Strangely, however, the customers were given no say about control of the National Curriculum, which was firmly centralised in the hands of the DES and the Secretary of State for Education. Indeed, perhaps the strangest aspect of the speedy introduction of the National Curriculum (and the continuing series of changes and modifications that have followed) was the lack of any significant rationale for the form it took, either in principle or in research evidence.

This is just one dramatic example of the recent deliberate redefinition of the traditional balance between autonomy, power and accountability in education in the English-speaking world. Both in the United States and in Australia there have been determined attempts to introduce explicit national (federal) curricula and modes of assessment against regional and professional opposition. In the 1980s such an overtly political wish to formulate or revise policies was driven by economic pressures, by cultural malaise and by growing suspicion of the professionalism of those involved in education. There was much negative media publicity throughout the English-speaking world suggesting that many schools and Higher Education institutions failed to give value for money, were not sufficiently accountable, and were underproductive. Such critical judgements of the past have not yet been accompanied by any coherent new policies for English, largely because of deep ambiguities within conservative thinking. There is a major tension between those committed to freedom of choice, individual rights and market forces and those pressing for strong authoritarian government, discipline and hierarchy. Detailed control of the English curriculum is clearly not compatible with the desire to provide greater variety and choice in education. So Michael Fallon, who was Parliamentary Under-Secretary of State in the DES 1990–2, during the establishment of the National Curriculum, could write in 1993 that 'It is time that the curriculum was handed back where it belongs – to the teachers' (*Independent on Sunday*, 21 November 1993).

Until quite recently, schools and universities in the UK thought of their educational role as lacking any real political dimension, and certainly as being outside the field of party politics. Administrative responsibility for education lay (in broad terms) with the government, but policy was implemented through the University Grants Committee (for universities) and through local authorities (for schools). The power of such intermediaries has now been seriously curtailed and placed in the hands of 'advisory' committees, hand-picked by the Secretary of State to ensure that only one viewpoint is ultimately heard. It is deeply destructive of morale when legislative changes in education (as in other public institutions like health, law and transport) can be forced through with no real discussion by whoever commands a majority in the House of Commons. The power of government to suppress dissent, if not to command agreement, has been seen in the way that policy is now being shaped.

Such political shaping has been clearly illustrated by successive attempts to replace Cox's original formulation of the English curriculum. Whatever weaknesses that document may have had, it had increasingly gained favour among teachers because it had built upon two decades of good practice in English teaching. It was acknowledged that there were three particular strengths in the Cox curriculum:

1 It was based upon the principle that language development combined the modes of speaking, reading and writing in equal measure and that development in any individual mode required the learner to understand through practice the relationship between language choice, purpose and audience. This made it a learner-centred curriculum which encouraged the development of a wide language repertoire for all pupils.
2 By preserving many of the fruits of English teachers' professional experience, it made it possible (in principle, at least) for the best practice of recent years to be maintained. It was compatible with those models of teaching – heavily supported by reflective English teachers – described in terms of the personal growth of the learner and cultural analysis of the uses of language.
3 Drama, media studies, information technology and knowledge about language were seen as integral to the main concerns of an English curriculum.

It must be added that when the Cox curriculum was translated into the mandatory Order of 1990 it also created many difficulties for teachers and implied some questionable practices (notably associated with the attempt to map language development to criteria for age-related levels of attainment which could not adequately be divided into those separate strands of achievement which the statements of attainment sought to describe). However, it was primarily the weaknesses in the practical implementation and assessment of the curriculum which caused major problems for schools. These were difficulties that had been foreseen by teachers in their responses to the consultative document but were ignored by the authorities in their rush to comply with government policy. Despite the increasingly fraught bureaucratic demands being made on them, teachers worked hard to implement the Cox curriculum, using their professional judgement to adapt, improve and redefine it where this seemed necessary. Research evidence from a study based at Warwick University and reports from English teaching associations suggested that early improvements were being seen (including increased teaching of 'great books' and 'more structured approaches to literacy', according to the *Times Educational Supplement*, 5 November 1993).

The increasing popularity of Cox within the profession ('left-wing extremists' and 'trendy educationists' according to the popular press) was itself seen in some political circles as a sign that the curriculum must be flawed ('English report fails the test', 'Thatcher furious with trendy experts'). The Centre for Policy Studies, the influential right-wing think-tank, had argued from 1988 onwards that the English curriculum was far too liberal in its conception of the subject. Its members joined with a strange mixture of others (proponents of phonics and graded readers, opponents of coursework assessment, pressure groups for streaming and selection) to claim that standards of literacy were falling, and to press for a revision that would be more in keeping with their views. The National Curriculum Council had a number of government appointees on its English panel who were highly sympathetic to this case and who were instrumental in recommending that a review should be undertaken. After the general election of 1992, the new Secretary of State for Education, John Patten, ignored the evidence in favour of Cox and called on the NCC to submit a formal review.

By a masterpiece of timing, the proposals for 'reforming' and 'improving' the curriculum were published in April 1993, just when the SATs boycott was gathering widespread support. They were greeted by overwhelming hostility within the profession and were swiftly followed by the resignation of a number of those associated with its production. There is little point in cataloguing the weaknesses of the 1993 proposals, but teachers were infuriated by a mechanistic emphasis on separate 'skills', a stress on word identification rather than meaning-making in early reading, the elimination of 'knowledge about language', a prescriptive reading curriculum, a heavy emphasis on Standard English, and the downgrading of drama and media studies. The consultation process recorded widespread alarm at the blatant narrowing of what was meant by 'English'. Antagonism was only defused by the disappearance of the NCC, the establishment of the Dearing Review, the withdrawal of assessment arrangements and the setting up of an English working party with an adequate representation of teachers.

## LOOKING AHEAD

What, if anything, have we learned from the past? English teachers have a robust tradition of contesting the nature of their own subject. The existence of several models of the subject as outlined in the opening chapter of the Cox Report only serves to underline this tradition. Indeed, that report gained much of its acceptance from the fact that it acknowledged the strengths of each model and attempted to create a curriculum which was 'broad church'. The work of influential individuals such as David Holbrook in the 1960s, James Britton and John Dixon in the 1970s, Andrew Wilkinson in the early 1980s, or of group projects like the Development of Writing Abilities, or the Oracy Project, or Language in the National Curriculum, serve to show the constant re-examination of the content and processes of the curriculum which has been carried out by teachers themselves.

English teachers as a body have never been opposed to the concept of a national curriculum. Indeed, much of the work of influential teachers in the 1980s such as David Jackson in his book *Continuity in English Teaching* (Jackson, 1983) argued for some form of coherence, balance and continuity across the full age range which would support the idea of entitlement for all pupils. However, National Curriculum documents, prescriptions and suggestions must be treated like any other professional advice and be judged by teachers who use their daily practice and experience as the chief yardstick of evaluation. The challenge is to reappraise what we already have, continually questioning our principles, policy and practice. As recent history (briefly sketched in this introduction) indicates, if we teachers do not do this, then the politicians will be only too happy to step in and do the redefining for us.

The quest for agreement over the curriculum has been bedevilled by the belief of politicians that there are simple answers to the complex problems of English teaching. Simplistic notions about English are particularly dangerous when they are used to influence the curriculum and assessment of schools. In contrast to the modish denigrating of professional opinion and research, we wish to insist that any policy should be grounded in experience and in evidence. The frank admissions of uncertainty in Cox's English Order were infinitely preferable to what was called in the 1993 version 'a clear definition of basic skills' but one which rested on shaky assumptions and ignored so much that we do know about talking, reading and writing. The quest for greater coherence does not necessarily imply a curriculum model that seeks to define what language features 'all' students at a given stage should know or be able to deploy. Simplistic ideas are still more dangerous when underpinning programmes of testing. The DfE has run an expensive advertising campaign to suggest to parents that National Curriculum testing will give them important information about their children's progress. In fact, though, teachers report that it gives little or no help in defining ability in writing, in assessing pupils or in diagnosing their needs. Testing is a highly political act. What precisely is to be tested, how, in what way, and for what audience and purpose? The people who are in a position to answer these questions – whether politicians, administrators, assessment specialists, theorists or teachers – exercise power over others. The two-year study at Warwick University suggests that it is national testing rather than the National Curriculum that has caused teachers to change their English teaching methods, not necessarily for the better. The report reflects the worries of teachers that, for example, children have been writing less and in shorter sentences because of the pressures of testing at 7. The notion that simple tests can be interpreted as 'proofs' that one school, teacher or region is more effective than another is both misguided and damaging to any who teach to such tests. By contrast, as suggested in the chapter on assessment, procedures must be devised that are derived from actual performance and that will be seen by teachers not as an external threat but as providing information that they and their students will find usable and helpful.

This book does not pretend to be a 'guide' to the National Curriculum. Such a guide would accept the view, which we contest, of a fixed text that simply needs to be explicated. What is read is much less important than how it is read and brought into being. Our concern is with the creative response which brings alive the curriculum in practice. We detect a two-sided challenge. On the one hand, the variant published versions and the accompanying debate challenge teachers to reassess their principles and practice in teaching English. On the other hand, experience in the classroom serves to challenge the practicality and good faith of the curriculum-makers. There has been a good deal of fuss about the need for teachers to be 'accountable', but there should be a balancing demand for accountability from those groups like SCAA and the DfE that feel able to make decisions vitally affecting teachers without ever publicly justifying them. The way in which the English subject group's proposals to Dearing were changed before publication – to the dismay and anger of English teachers in that group and in the advisory team for KS1 – is just one more example of the disagreements and conflicting values that have continued ever since the original draft of the Cox Report was printed. It has always been clear that irreconcilable views exist about such topics as initial literacy, the relative importance of spoken Standard English, the role of cultural and media studies, the meaning of 'knowledge about language', bilingualism, and the concept of a literary canon. We do not suggest that English teachers should be the only people with a right to an opinion on these subjects. However, it is surely objectionable when undebated changes are made by unknown hands, and privileged by being printed without any discussion, as though representing the agreed views of the working party.

The lesson of these recent years is surely that a rigid mandatory curriculum for English is a nonsense because consensus is impossible to achieve; there will be endless wrangling by groups wanting change because their particular views seem unrepresented and by Secretaries of State with different priorities. Instead we need a framework for the curriculum that is flexible enough not to rule out any sensible inter-pretation of English for ages 5 to 16. In fact, the slimline *English in the National Curriculum* (DFE/HMSO, 1995), seems to us to come quite close to that. It has abandoned any pretence of being a syllabus and simply offers a basis or broad check-list for departments' own schemes of work. The discretionary element makes clear that a National Curriculum can only provide part of a pupil's entitlement. The principle in The Dearing Report that more should be left to the professional judgement of teachers has been upheld, particularly in the abandonment of trivial itemised assessment. In the compromises that have marked the latest version, compared with the draft proposals of 1994, we can welcome the stress on the integration of the English modes, the reordering of programmes of study to emphasise function and range, the greater emphasis on 'opportunities' (and the soft-pedalling of 'should be taught') and language diversity, the strengthening of media studies and drama, and the more balanced treatment of phonics and of Standard English. The more manageable level descriptions implicitly acknowledge the inadequacy of standardised testing. Global judgements about pupils' use of their abilities in talking, reading and writing are seen to be inevitably personal and impressionistic. Few elements in the programmes of study can be objected to in themselves; it is up to teachers to modify what seem to them questionable emphases, interpretations or omissions. Just as the Cox curriculum was 'realised' in very different ways in different schools, so any new version of the English curriculum will equally be transformed, modified and partially ignored in practice. Whatever the documents may say, eventually teachers have to shut the classroom door and get on with the real business of English. The irony is that in the ten years since the first, ill-received official critique (*The English Curriculum 5–16*, 1984) and after endless committees, working parties and agitation, we are now back with a set of proposals for English that is hardly different from what was being practised in most schools at the beginning of that period. Has it all been worth it? The only clear result has been the politicising of English teachers and their increased suspicion of those who seek to manipulate them.

The challenge and opportunity now is for teachers to abandon the nightmare of following mechanically some set of imposed tasks and to begin responding personally and critically to the endlessly changing task of framing policy for English. This will involve skills of interpretation, discrimination and judgement (even perhaps deconstruction) in comparing the different and discrepant attempts at a National Curriculum and relating them to a school's existing practice. It should then be possible to identify priorities (what are we teaching English *for*? how does learning go on through language?) rather than trying to tick off endless items on some impersonal list of mechanical 'skills'. It will mean identifying differences of opinion that exist within a department, and considering how far this variety is a strength and how far it may cause problems. A curriculum has to be flexible enough to allow teachers with different skills and interests to make different contributions, rather than assuming that all should offer the same second-hand diet. It will mean being able to justify agreed positions and principles, especially where they may seem to conflict with official policy. It should imply keeping in touch with other

schools and areas through teachers' groups and professional organisations like the National Association for the Teaching of English. In other
words, English teachers should continue to act pragmatically as they have
always done, holding fast to their principles but otherwise evolving in
changing circumstances.

The chapters in this book are attempts to consider how particular
aspects of a national curriculum can be reconciled with the best practice
of the English teaching tradition. They have been written by teachers
working under the pressure of continually shifting official policies, but
attempting to look beyond the immediate towards the lessons of the past
for the next decade. The questions posed in the chapter titles are those
raised by teachers in in-service workshops as issues which most concern
them. The different contributions to this book suggest that it is perfectly
possible to comply with the statutory requirements of a central curriculum and yet to maintain most of what has been won in the daily experience
of hundreds of effective English teachers over the last decades.

## REFERENCES

Board of Education (1910) *The Teaching of English in Secondary Schools*, HMSO
Cox, B (1990) Editorial, *Critical Quarterly*, Vol. 32, No. 4, pp. 1–6
Dearing, R (1993) *The National Curriculum and its Assessment: An Interim Report*,
    NCC and SEAC
DES (1989) *English for Ages 5 to 16*, HMSO
DES/WO (1990) *English in the National Curriculum*, HMSO
DFE (1993) *English for Ages 5 to 16*, HMSO
DFE (1995) *English in the National Curriculum*, HMSO
HMI (1984) *English for Ages 5 to 16*, DES
HMI (1986) *English for Ages 5 to 16: The Responses*, DES
Jackson, D (1983) *Continuity in English Teaching*, Methuen, London
NCC (1993) *National Curriculum Council Consultation Report: English in the National
    Curriculum*, NCC, York
Protherough, R and Atkinson, J (1991) *The Making of English Teachers*, Open
    University Press, Buckingham
SCAA (1994) *English in the National Curriculum: Draft Proposals*, Schools Curricu-
    lum and Assessment Authority

# Chapter 2

# Can we raise the standard of speaking and listening?

*John Johnson*

Ten years ago the place of the spoken word in English teaching was fairly clear. Although most teachers had increased their awareness of its importance in the curriculum, and the old CSE boards had recognised its importance by including it in their syllabuses, it was not often prominent in English departments' priorities for development, and it featured in very few GCE O-level syllabuses (this being a 'higher' status qualification than CSE). It would have been hard to believe that it would become a statutory and compulsory part of every pupil's curriculum, and it would have stretched the imagination to believe that national controversy would surround it to the extent that it became the subject of prime ministerial speeches!

There are many people who could legitimately claim to have played a role in the development of talk in the English curriculum in the past twenty years or so – James Britton, Douglas Barnes, Andrew Wilkinson, Harold Rosen, Alan Howe, to name but five prominent English specialists whose role in changing and improving the teaching and learning of speaking and listening could be clearly defined. For me, however, it was Sir Keith Joseph who above all others can claim to have put speaking and listening into the centre of modern developments in English teaching. As Secretary of State for Education in the early 1980s he surprised many by arguing strongly that teachers should pay attention to developing and improving children's oral work:

> It will in my view be desirable to examine how the use of oral work . . .
> might be encouraged in the teaching of all subjects.
> (31 January 1984, letter to Professor Roger Blin-Stoyle, the Chairman
> of SCDC, the new School Curriculum Development Committee)

But he also insisted that oral communication should feature as a particular part in all the new GCSE English syllabuses, insisting that it be assessed on a grade scale of 1 to 5 and appearing on all candidates' examination certificates as a separate result.

Brian Cox, who was invited by a later Secretary of State, Kenneth

Baker, to chair the English Working Group for the development of English in the National Curriculum, also surprised the English teaching world by endorsing Keith Joseph's views, and recommending that the development of speaking and listening should feature as one-third of the English curriculum, within an Attainment Target (AT1) which was defined in the two Statutory Orders (DES, 1989 and 1990) that laid down the Curriculum as 'The development of pupils' understanding of the spoken word and the capacity to express themselves effectively in a variety of speaking and listening activities, matching style and response to audience and purpose.' The Working Group's proposals were endorsed by the Secretary of State in these Orders.

The Orders also laid down detailed content for the Programmes of Study and the Levels and Statements of Attainment which were to be constituent parts of the Attainment Target itself. They contained requirements which were broad and wide ranging, demanding that pupils engage in activities which were stimulating and challenging, and in which there was a variety of purpose or role for them. Brian Cox's group explained the background to and the thinking behind the Orders in two reports which accompanied the Working Group's proposals. These reports summarised the Group's thinking on other matters such as assessment, linguistic diversity, knowledge about language and Standard English. Standard English was envisaged as relevant to some children in the primary school (those working towards level 5) and was placed firmly on the agenda of secondary English teachers by being required at level 6 and beyond. It is a matter to which I shall return later in this chapter.

During the period of the preparation and first implementation of English in the National Curriculum, I was fortunate enough to be the Director of the National Oracy Project, which the SCDC had set up in response to Sir Keith Joseph's call. We were asked to prepare publications for the National Curriculum Council (NCC), which took on SCDC's role, to help teachers to implement the Orders. We did this first through a series of publications called *Teaching, Talking and Learning* (NCC, 1989, 1990a, 1990b). We summarised the requirements of AT1 Speaking and Listening and other aspects of the National Curriculum as follows:

| What? (Uses) | How? (Activities) | Where? (Contexts) |
|---|---|---|
| • Expressing feelings and opinions about themselves, the subject or activity | • Preparing presentations to class/school/parents | • Across curriculum areas, e.g. the science laboratory, the technology room |
| • Taking part in group discussions. Presenting ideas, information, texts | • Planning and designing tasks, and setting and solving problems within them | • In a variety of groupings (paired, single-sex, small-group, class, with/without presence of teacher) |
| • Interpreting arguments and developing them | • Identifying specific outcomes for their own work | |

- Discriminating between fact and opinion
- Summarising views to gain a consensus
- Instructing and responding to instructions
- Conveying information
- Role play
- Reflecting upon their own talk and learning the talk of others
- Exploratory talk (predicting, speculating, hypothesising)
- Demonstrating knowledge of language

- Making and testing hypotheses
- Reporting and discussing stories, poems, plays and other texts
- Reasoning and arguing
- Using talk in shared reading or writing activity
- Simulations and group drama
- Discussing and analysing language in use

- In contact with audiences beyond the classroom
- In representative roles, acting on behalf of others
- Using audio/video, radio, television, telephone, computer
- In enquiry and survey work in the locality or on field visits/trips
- In mini-enterprise, work shadowing or industry liaison exercises

We found that few teachers were accustomed to planning for the massive range of uses, activities and contexts required in the Orders. Many were uncertain of the extent or the quality of children's talk both in their own classrooms and across the school. And although GCSE English syllabuses had led to more organised, if often quite formal, talk in the later years of secondary schooling, in the earlier years (those associated with Key Stage 3) there was little detailed attention to such matters as 'assess and interpret arguments' or 'give increasingly precise instructions'.

Although there were immediate difficulties with implementing these Orders, then, many teachers were sufficiently encouraged to face up to the challenges. And by and large they were successful in improving the standards of their students' work in this area of the curriculum. An HMI Report (DES, 1992) on National Curriculum English indicated that in 1991:

> Standards in Speaking and Listening were high. Eighty per cent was rated satisfactory including nearly half which was good. In good oral work pupils made extended, thoughtful contributions and built on points made by others. They contributed willingly, in well structured Standard English, and were able to question, listen and explain. They learnt to take turns, to speak with confidence, and to debate. Some were clearly responding well to challenges which had been carefully structured to conform to National Curriculum requirements. It was also more apparent that pupils of modest attainment were pushed to their personal limits in such oral work.

Within the National Oracy Project it was possible to publicise some of the most successful approaches to developing and improving speaking and listening, and to identify the best classroom activities, because hundreds of teachers were keeping records of students' work, and meeting regularly to compare notes. The rest of this chapter summarises some of these approaches under a number of separate headings.

## INVESTIGATING TALK

It was important to identify starting points, both for teachers and for students. So in many classes teachers set about answering such questions as these:

• Who talks, where, what about? Is it related to work?
• Do some children use other language in school?
• Are there differences between boys and girls?
• Is that quiet child always so reticent?
• What sorts of talk happen at different activities?
• What about my own talk? Do I listen?
• What are my pupils' attitudes to talk?
• What is happening when groups are working together, without me present?

To find answers to their questions, the teachers gathered evidence in a variety of ways:

• they observed individual children at intervals during a day or week, jotting down details of where the child was, what was being said or done, and why;
• they tape-recorded groups of children working together;
• they recorded themselves working with a group, the whole class or individual children;
• they asked pupils about their perceptions of talk;
• they recorded or observed talk in particular curriculum areas or areas of the classroom;
• they 'followed' a pupil for a day, noting or recording the talk activities of a whole day.

Many of the things which the teachers found out surprised them. Their students were very perceptive about the issues which surround talk in classroom – its low status, teachers' associations of talk with pupils becoming distracted and wandering 'off-task', the primacy of the teacher's voice – and many had negative views about their own accents and dialects, and about their own performance in the spoken word.

## GETTING TALK GOING

As a consequence, teachers looked for ways of 'getting things going' in the classroom, so that students would have a variety of purposes and roles in their discussions, and would value talk more highly. Some approaches were borrowed or adapted from innovative approaches to learning being developed in the USA or Australia. This is a summary of some of the approaches which proved popular with teachers:

## BRAINSTORMING

A large group, or even the whole class, will contribute ideas, or thoughts, or words, off the top of their heads, related to a particular subject or problem. All contributions are listed without comment, and then the students use their list to select tasks or topics for further work. Smaller groups, even pairs, can also gather thoughts in this way. This activity is particularly valuable at the start of a lesson, when the students' own ideas can be gathered and subsequently used by both teacher and students during the lesson.

## JIGSAW

This is an extremely effective form of co-operative learning. A topic is set and subdivided into areas. 'Home Groups' are formed, and each child in the Home Group is given one of the topic areas in which to become an 'expert'. The child then joins prospective 'experts' in the same area from the other Home Groups, to form an 'expert group'. Each expert group works on its chosen area, and then the members return to their Home Groups to make a report and to share in putting their whole set of discoveries together. Each 'Home Group' can then present its work to others. Jigsawing gives all children a key role to play in the work of a group, and teachers have found it an especially effective way of encouraging students to take on new and challenging activities such as exploring new texts or poems without feeling that their tentative or exploratory ideas are being too exposed to others' criticism.

## TWOS TO FOURS

Children work together in pairs, perhaps upon a particular problem or task. They then join another pair to explain what they have achieved, and to compare this with the work of the other pair. This provides a valuable opportunity to express understanding, and to respond to the views of others in a supportive context. As with other activities, it can give a genuine purpose to the communication between the students.

## RAINBOW GROUPS

A way of ensuring that children experience working alongside a range of others is to give each child in a group a number, or a colour. When the group has worked together, all the students of the same number or colour form new groups to compare what they have done. If all groups have the task of preparing a presentation on one part of the topic, the rainbow groups can then put together the final presentation, knowing that each member of any group will have had a thorough preparation.

## ENVOYS

Often, in group work, the teacher is concerned that he or she will be under pressure from many different directions. Envoying helps students to find help and support without necessarily having recourse to the teacher. If a group needs to check something, or to obtain information, one of the group can be sent as an 'envoy' to the library, or resource centre, or another group, and will then report back. Another use is to ask groups to send an envoy to a different group to explain what they have done, obtain responses and suggestions, and bring them back to the group.

## LISTENING TRIADS

This strategy encourages students, in groups of three, to take on the roles of talker, questioner, or recorder. The talker explains or comments on an issue or activity. The questioner prompts and seeks clarification. The recorder makes notes, and at the end of the (brief) time gives a report of the conversation. Next time the roles are changed. This is a very useful strategy for getting informal presentations done by a whole class in a relatively limited amount of time.

## CRITICAL FRIENDS

A group member is responsible for observing the ways in which the group works together. Using a simple guide list (which students can devise), the observer watches and listens as the students work. The information is then discussed by the group. This helps students to develop their own evaluative strategies, and enables the teacher to introduce the criteria by which more formal assessment may take place.

## CHANGING THE ROLE OF THE TEACHER

By introducing students to more purposeful talk in this way, teachers found that their own role in the classroom changed. If they no longer needed at all times to be leading the whole class, it was possible to take on other roles. These can be summarised as follows:

| | |
|---|---|
| *Organiser:* | Would you like to form six groups of four? |
| *Provider:* | You might find what you need in the Library. |
| *Supporter:* | Let me know if you want me to work with you. |
| *Arbiter:* | Try and make sure that you've heard from everyone before you reach a decision. |
| *Collaborator:* | Perhaps we need to look at it another way. |
| *Working group member:* | What would you like me to do? |
| *Director:* | All groups will need to report back in half an hour. |
| *Editor:* | Where will this fit in? |
| *Friend:* | Are you feeling a bit better about the work today? |
| *Adviser:* | Have you considered any alternatives? |
| *Learner:* | I never knew that before. |
| *Expert:* | The other useful information is in the pamphlet. |
| *Listener:* | Mmm . . . mmm . . . go on . . . this is very interesting. |

Of course, the shift in teaching role had to be balanced by shifting expectations of the roles that children could fulfil. They could, for example, develop the confidence and self-esteem to take risks, to offer tentative thoughts, to make exploratory statements and to offer hypothetical avenues for potential investigation and evaluation. They could also consider ideas and materials put before them, formulate questions for themselves, negotiate the ground rules and develop a sense of ownership over the learning process.

## EQUAL OPPORTUNITIES IN TALK

Not all students found it easy to respond to the increased demand on them to participate and to engage actively in talk in the classroom. It was necessary, not least because of the notion of 'entitlement' behind the National Curriculum itself, to ensure that all pupils had the fullest possible access to speaking and listening activities. Teachers' investigations revealed a host of inequalities. Boys and girls, for example, may have different experiences of and attitudes to talk, hold different expectations of their role in talk, and therefore need the teacher on occasion to use different strategies in the classroom. In particular, boys may refuse to work with girls, may adopt the role of 'expert' or leader in group discussions, may be reluctant to talk sensitively or to express emotion, and may subject girls to verbal harassment. Girls may adopt non-speaking or subservient roles in group conversations, and may find it difficult to get equal shares of teachers' time and attention.

Some strategies for overcoming these problems are:

- allow girls to choose other girls to work with at times;
- give girls active and responsible roles in discussions;
- help boys to listen by giving them some of the evaluative and responsive roles;
- negotiate with the students what the ground rules for the discussion should be;
- encourage the students to take turns;
- value and praise any evidence of listening and constructive response;
- talk with the students about what makes talk successful.

Teachers have found that they too could be subject to the subtle and often subconscious attitudes towards talk which affect all in society. For example, their assessments of children's talk could be affected by subconscious bias or prejudice. There are dangers that teachers would give undue credit to boys for responsive listening, for good eye contact with other speakers, for supportive questioning or for building on others' contributions simply because these were unexpected features of boys' talk, and not ascribe the same value to these features of girls' talk.

Although there are complex and difficult issues for teachers to address, many found it a valuable professional challenge to investigate. Identifying the hitherto unrevealed problems experienced by students helped them to enhance their professional understanding and practice in a way which benefited their students. The same was true for teachers of children with special needs, where extra care and attention is necessary to enable children to participate fully in lessons. Among the strategies found to be successful were:

- pairing pupils with supportive partners;
- putting pupils into the role of questioner and interviewer;
- planning for well-structured small-group work, with clear time limits;
- asking for appropriate teacher interaction in small-group work;
- tape-recording individual pupils doing their tasks, using a microphone where necessary;
- providing pupils with a cassette player so that they can record their work orally rather than in writing;
- reducing extraneous noise and explaining tasks very fully and explicitly;
- using drama, role play, puppets and play to encourage participatory talk.

In general, teachers found it important to separate issues of special needs from issues concerned with linguistic diversity. There was always too much danger that bilingual pupils, or children with strong regional dialects, would be described as having 'problems'. It was better to consider such pupils as possessing linguistic strengths, which needed to be encouraged and nurtured. The following principles appeared to support this:

- pupils' home languages should be respected;
- displays and resources should reflect the cultures and contexts in which children's languages are used;
- all children's languages should be encouraged in presentations and public contexts such as school assemblies;
- all children's languages should as far as possible be reflected in the curriculum;
- assessment of pupils' work should not be affected adversely by any comparative weakness in English.

## ASSESSMENT OF TALK AND ASSESSMENT THROUGH TALK

Alongside their introduction of the programmes of study of the National Curriculum, teachers also had to commence assessing their students' progress in each Attainment Target. This involved setting up systems for determining whether or not students had provided to their teachers sufficient evidence of achievement of the individual Statements of Attainment in each Attainment Target. For most teachers this resulted in a large-scale exercise of gathering evidence, recording progress and achievement, weighing these records against Statements of Attainment, and making a judgement of students' level of attainment on the ten-point scale which had been introduced by government. Guidance for this was given to teachers by the government's agency, the School Examinations and Assessment Council, which came to define the process of assessment – sometimes termed 'criterion-referencing' – as a rather atomistic and fragmentary process, in which curriculum activities were planned with specific Statements of Attainment in mind, and teachers' observations of their pupils at work were undertaken with these specific Statements, or criteria, in mind.

Teachers had already found assessing speaking and listening to be innovative, demanding and problematic. For a start, talk is simply an unfamiliar medium for teachers to use in assessment. The methods which they have used to conduct written assessment, and particularly the kinds of tasks set for written assessment, are often wholly inappropriate for oral assessment. And there are additional problems in observing talk – where teachers often experience initial uncertainty about what exactly they are looking at – and in capturing talk so that it can be considered in any objective terms. Also, the approaches to assessment recommended by SEAC did not take account of the fact that students' talk often strayed outside the parameters set by the Statements of Attainment into a different kind of talk altogether.

Yet teachers also found that if assessment were not considered by the demands of literacy, many pupils were better enabled to show what they 'know, understand and can do'. Through observing and listening to pupils at work, teachers got much fuller access to the processes of learning, not just the final outcomes. And assessment could be genuinely formative if teachers could observe the first stages of a piece of work to check that the pupils both understood the task and had the required knowledge. We must draw one crucial distinction, however, between two kinds of oral assessment:

### Assessment of talk

Assessment of talk is assessment of pupils' *use of spoken language*, especially their English. It looks particularly at such features of speaking and listening as appropriateness, diction, presentation, tone, register, responsiveness, interpersonal skills, and so on. In the National Curriculum it will lead to assessment of the attainment target and profile component Speaking and Listening.

### Assessment through talk

Assessment through talk is an assessment of *the knowledge and understanding of a subject*, displayed by pupils through their talk. It looks particularly at such features as accuracy, use of diction and terminology, quantity and quality of knowledge and understanding, application of these to a new situation, and so on. In the National Curriculum it can lead to assessment in any subject area, including the attainment targets for Reading and Writing in English.

Teachers also found it important to remember that:

- When children and adults speak, they do not always make their knowledge explicit (like an iceberg, the greater proportion remains hidden).
- Pupils may find it hard to 'display' all their knowledge in conversation with teachers when they know that their teachers are more expert than they are.
- A misunderstanding of the task, or a difficult relationship between pupils, may prevent them showing all that they do through talk.

At times, therefore, teachers found that oral work would not produce valid evidence, and they needed simply to discount what they had observed, because it would not stand as valid evidence of pupils' achievements.

For these reasons, it was necessary to develop models of assessment which involved collecting information about children's oral work over a wide range of contexts and over a period of time, and which involved the pupils and teachers in discussing and reflecting on the information collected. The information particularly concentrated on the children's best, most interesting or most noteworthy oral work, often described as 'catching them peaking'.

## CHANGING THE ORDERS

Although teachers had responded positively to the new English curriculum, in speaking and listening as in other areas, it started to become apparent in 1991 that a number of 'right-wing' political or quasi-educational agencies or individuals were not content with either the curriculum itself or with the progress made by schools in raising standards. The influence of such bodies as the Centre for Policy Studies has been documented elsewhere – see for example a publication by the National Association for the Teaching of English, *Made Tongue-tied by Authority* (1992) – but its views started to prevail in the National Curriculum Council itself. Defying the evidence of HMI, the NCC published in July 1992 advice to the Secretary of State entitled *National Curriculum English: the Case for Revising the Order*. Among the assertions made by the NCC was the view that 'The current Order does not . . . place sufficient emphasis on the requirement that all pupils . . . should become confident users of standard English. Neither does it stress the need for pupils to develop skills of close and attentive listening.' The Secretary of State accepted this advice, and NCC commenced a process of developing a new proposed Order, the publication of which (DFE, 1993) by the government started a fierce political and educational debate in schools, in the political arena and in the media.

It is important to note the difficulties which the government's demands concerning spoken Standard English place on teachers. For a start, there is not a clear agreement either in the educational world or in the academic world of linguistics about what does or does not constitute spoken Standard English. The NCC pursued several definitions in the period after its advice (above), but by September 1993 (NCC, 1993) was only prepared to state that it contained a limited number of 'core grammatical features', while recognising that it differed from written Standard English in a 'small number of grammatical and lexical ways'. With deliberate understatement (one assumes) the NCC stated that spoken Standard English may contain 'unfinished or recast sentences which would be avoided by a writer in a polished piece'. Second, insisting that students who speak any dialect of non-Standard English suddenly switch to speaking spoken Standard English may be positively ruinous of teacher–student relationships and of students' confidence in the classroom. And third, there is as yet little published information for teachers on how best to develop students' abilities in speaking spoken Standard English.

These difficulties for teachers were actually increased by the emphasis of the 1994 draft proposals, where the requirement that 'pupils should be taught to use the vocabulary and grammar of spoken standard English' is placed first, before more basic needs like formulating and clarifying ideas, adapting to context or listening and responding to others. The 1993 programme of study for KS1 introduced the suggestion that children 'should be introduced with appropriate sensitivity to the basic conventions of Standard English' as the fourth point in a six-item list that began with concerns for story-telling, efficient discussion, clarity and effectiveness. In 1994 'growing appreciation of the significance of standard English' is given new priority as the first item on the list. Similarly, instead of seeing the awareness of Standard English as just one aspect of language study (as was intended by the English working group), the printed version that emerged from SCAA headed that section at each key stage *Standard English and Language Study*. It also removed items that referred to children as speakers 'of more than one variety of English' or that asked them to 'consider some of the differences in vocabulary and grammar between Standard and non-Standard varieties'.

The actual details of the key skills and of the activities to be practised, offered in the 1993 and 1994 proposals, incorporate much of what was best in the previous Orders and provide in general a better definition of a worthwhile 'entitlement curriculum' in oral language. There are aspects in which positive development has taken place. Elements concerned with the development of evaluation and reflection are one example. Another is the improvement in the hierarchy of knowledge about language (apart from the damaging shift of emphasis mentioned above).

The major and most welcome improvement in the slimmed-down 1994 proposals has been in assessment. Secondary schools had found it difficult to use the original Statements of Attainment to allocate children's talk confidently to different levels. In 1993 the advice from the government's agency (the School Examinations and Assessment Council) was greeted with derision. The booklet *Children's Work Assessed in Key Stage 3*, for example, described the process by which certain children's talk was to be assessed but, contrary to the very title of the publication, gave teachers no examples of children's work whatsoever. An earlier publication, a video of children talking, which would have helped teachers to understand the process better, was scrapped by SEAC. The 1993 Statements of Attainment awkwardly separated 'communication' from 'listening and responding'. In striving to follow the ten-level format they made unreal distinctions, as between speaking 'fluently' (8), 'imaginatively' (9), 'with flair, creativity and spontaneity' (10) or listening 'carefully', 'constructively', 'with sustained concentration' and so on. The brief descriptions of the 1994 proposals, by contrast, attempted to be more helpful and down to earth, and were certainly more straightforward to apply.

The central issue for teachers is whether the 1994 proposals, with their undeniable improvements of previous versions of the oral curriculum, are adequate to guide their work towards the next century. They will be concerned at an emphasis on uniformity that seems intolerant of diversity, that largely ignores bilingualism, and that implicitly (by defining differences in terms of the complexity of topics discussed) seems hostile to patterns of class organisation which mix pupils of different abilities together. In these respects, the government and its advisers would do well to practise level 10 ability and 'listen with sensitivity and discrimination'.

## REFERENCES

DES (1989) *English in the National Curriculum* and (1990) *English in the National Curriculum No 2*, HMSO

DES (1992) *English Key Stages 1, 2, and 3, a Report by Her Majesty's Inspectorate*, HMSO

DFE (1993) *English for Ages 5 to 16*, HMSO

NATE (1992) *Made Tongue-tied by Authority, New Orders for English?*, Longman, Harlow

NCC (1989) *Teaching, Talking and Learning Key Stage One*, (1990a) *Teaching and Learning Key Stage Two*, (1990b) *Teaching and Learning Key Stage Three*, NCC, York. Available only from The National Association for the Teaching of English

NCC (1993) *Consultation Report on English*, NCC, York

SCAA (1994) *English in the National Curriculum: Draft Proposals (May 1994)*, Schools Curriculum & Assessment Authority

# Chapter 3

# What is a reading curriculum?

*Robert Protherough*

What is a *national* reading curriculum meant to be and to do? What are its legitimate concerns? What help in their work might English teachers reasonably expect from it? What relationship does it bear to the actual reading programme being followed in a particular school?

Sir Ron Dearing's review of the curriculum invited us to look critically at three distinct attempts to answer these questions in defining *English for Ages 5 to 16* (DES, 1989; DFE, 1993; SCAA, 1994) and to reconsider our own policies and practice. As readers, we have all approached those yellow and white pages with our own acquired reading styles; we respond to them in the context of our current situation and in the light of our own histories, experiences and prejudices. In the act of reading, we each of us construct our own 'text' and act upon it. The only real value of any national curriculum lies in this activity: the response of teachers that leads to effective action.

A national reading curriculum should provide us with the means to think about four main topics:

- the nature of the reading process (and more specifically the purposes of reading in school);
- the principles by which materials for reading should be selected;
- the definition of what constitutes 'progress' or 'development' in reading;
- the role of the teacher in encouraging and monitoring this progress.

The bulk of this chapter examines what the curriculum documents so far offered have to say about these four topics and considers what English teachers might use, what they should ignore and what supplementary thinking of their own will be required. No national curriculum can pretend to offer a set of recipes to be taken over ready-made in every school, regardless of their differences. A curriculum should not pretend to be a syllabus; it should not be concerned with specifying in detail either what is to be read or what teaching methods are to be practised. Such areas should be the professional concern of the teachers charged to 'deliver' the curriculum. Nor should its framework be dictated by the need for testing; the curriculum should drive its assessment, not the other way round.

## THE NEED FOR AN AGREED READING CURRICULUM

The openly political origins of the National Curriculum should not obscure the fact that there was already clear professional consensus about the need for greater coherence in policy and planning, particularly at secondary level. This had been prompted in part by changes in public examinations (the coming of GCSE and new courses at A-level) but more significantly by changes within the thinking of English teachers. Three of these, concerned in particular with reading, deserve consideration.

## 1. DISSATISFACTION WITH THE BROKEN-BACKED CURRICULUM

Virtually all of those involved in schooling – teachers, students and inspectors – had become disturbed about the lack of continuity in the reading experiences on offer at secondary level. Teachers expressed alarm at the apparent failures in cross-phase understanding and in comparing reading experiences at different ages. The majority of students at every stage up to university said they felt unprepared for the different reading demands facing them (Protherough, 1989). This was also a recurrent note in the HMI report of summer 1989, concluding that practice was 'not underpinned by sufficiently clear, coherent and comprehensive reading policies or organisation' (HMI, 1989, para 62).

## 2. A WISH TO TAKE INTO ACCOUNT IMPROVED UNDERSTANDING OF THE WAYS IN WHICH INDIVIDUALS DEVELOP AS READERS

Teachers have increasingly been led to look for signs of development in the reading abilities of their children, relating small-scale studies of their own and of others to the tentative models that have been advanced. There has been general acknowledgement that policies for reading at secondary level have to be based on a view of how children come to be more capable and effective readers, and of how the school can cater for different abilities and needs.

## 3. THE NEED FOR REDEFINITION POSED BY NEW APPROACHES TO TEACHING

Views of reading, of teaching methods and of assessment are inseparably bound up together. The movement away from, say, reading round the class, comprehension tests and line-by-line explication of what set texts 'mean', with their underlying assumption that everyone is sharing the same reading experience, has meant looking for alternative structures to underpin the curriculum. The 'individualising' of reading, associated with activities like the making of consecutive responses, prediction and retrospection, reframing and recreating texts, has demanded clearer departmental agreement about how these activities build cumulatively at different stages.

There has thus been overwhelming support for the *idea* of a national curriculum; the form it should take has been more contentious. Perhaps the major benefit to be gained from the debate has been the focus it has given to concerns like the three outlined above. However, educational success or failure turns on what happens in the nation's schools.

Do the proposals help them to achieve the aims expressed, and specifically:

- to devise more coherent policies and programmes for reading, based on a credible model of the reading process;
- to offer better provision of books and other materials;
- to 'translate' Programmes of Study into actual schemes of work;
- to understand 'development' better in terms of students' actual reading and response,
- to monitor as well as simply to encourage private reading;
- to improve ways of diagnosing the kinds of help that individuals need?

## THE READING PROCESS AND 'LEARNING TO READ'

How plainly can a national document say what reading is all about? It is fascinating to consider the particular language chosen to express the aims of the programme of study in the published versions:

> The development of the ability to read, understand and respond to all types of writing; the development of reading and information-retrieval strategies for the purposes of study; the development of knowledge about language.
>
> (DES, 1989)

> The development of the ability to read accurately, widely and fluently, encountering texts of increasing complexity, including those central to our literary heritage, as well as from other cultures and traditions.
>
> (DFE, 1993)

> The development of the ability to read, understand and respond to a wide range of literary and non-literary texts.
>
> (DFE, 1993, Welsh Office version)

The development of pupils' reading. Pupils should be taught to:

- read accurately and fluently;
- understand and respond to literature of increasing complexity drawn from the English literary heritage and from other cultures and traditions;
- analyse and evaluate a wide range of texts.

(SCAA, 1994)

In the first, the purpose of reading is seen as a matter of the student's understanding and response; in the second these are omitted in favour of judgements (by the teacher?) about accuracy and fluency. The first links reading to studying and to wider awareness of language; the second emphasises texts rather than readers, and introduces the judgement about those seen (by whom?) as 'central to our literary heritage' (tactfully quoting a phrase used by the Secretary of State himself in commissioning the review). The fourth version essentially reshapes the second and adds a clause about analysis and evaluation. The third, Welsh, version is briefest and probably best. It is perhaps significant that none of the four uses the first verb in the separate Scottish curriculum statement: 'to *enjoy* and respond to a variety of texts' (Scottish Education Department, 1990).

There is a similar difference in emphasis about learning and teaching, as well as in tone and attitude, when dealing with the process of learning to read. The earlier version stressed motivation throughout:

> the pleasure principle should motivate the programmes of study, and always be given high priority' (16.4). No methods or resources or teaching styles can 'deliver' improvements in literacy unless pupils want to use reading for their own purposes and pleasures.

> It is a prerequisite of successful teaching of reading, especially in the early stages, that whenever techniques are taught, or books are chosen for children's use, meaning should always be in the foreground. (16.2)

The 1993 notes on Attainment Target 2 opened with the intentions:

- to identify the essential knowledge and skills involved in learning to read . . .
- to define the nature and development of more advanced reading skills. (6.6)

Accordingly, the proposals for Key Stage 1 began with the assertion:

> Pupils learn to read when they are taught the necessary skills, of which phonics is an essential component. (p. 28)

This is one of a number of shifts of emphasis from what students should learn to prescribing what and how teachers should teach, what 'pupils need to be taught'. Indeed, throughout the 1993 volume ran an almost obsessive concern for 'precision' in the 'definition' of 'skills'. No evidence was given for this conviction that teaching will be better and that standards will improve if we can define certain discrete 'skills' more precisely and identify what methods will best result in acquiring them. 'More explicit definition' seems to lead, with no supporting argument, towards 'statutory requirement'. Accordingly the 1993 Attainment Targets broke down global abilities into separate testable scraps. By contrast, the 1989 Order offered a model of the reading process as unitary, 'not a set of discrete skills which can be taught separately in turn and, ultimately, bolted together' (16.9).

The examples above (and others that readers may identify) indicate that the 1993 proposals did not – as the authors claimed – simply revise the 1989 Cox Order, building on its strengths. They offered a radically different view of what reading is and of how it should be taught in schools. The 1995 Orders placed the 'key skills' in bottom-up order, starting with 'phonic knowledge' and ending with 'contextual understanding'. However, in a helpful shift of emphasis, the skills were preceded by sections requiring 'extensive experience of children's literature', material that would 'stimulate pupils' imagination', and an emphasis on developing 'understanding of the nature and purpose of reading'. Faced by these variations, English departments will need to decide (and to record) for themselves how they intend to define and to justify their particular view of the reading process and of the school's responsibility for helping students in the lifelong process of learning to read.

## WHAT IS TO BE READ?

What help does a national curriculum provide for English departments that are planning their reading programmes? All versions require students to be encouraged in the reading of 'an increasingly wide range and variety of texts'. Whose responsibility is it to choose those texts and on what basis is that choice to be made?

Literature constitutes itself through a variety of non-literary institutional forms: the publishing network, the education system, the public examination bodies, the media, and so on. Students' perceptions of literature are largely defined by the authors and texts that have been nominated by someone else as valuable for being studied, taught and examined, and the works in fashion at any time continually change (Protherough, 1986, pp. 70–1, 96–7, 123–4). In the 1960s and 1970s, the shift away from a selective system towards almost universal comprehensive education, the raising of the school leaving age, the extension of external examinations to cater for the great majority of pupils and the increasing popularity of mixed-ability teaching all demanded a reappraisal of the texts on offer in schools. The range became more international, widened in theme and genre, and included more 'popular' materials, drawing increasingly on television, films, newspapers and songs. The concept of 'literature' as an unproblematic category, a fixed hierarchy of 'quality', was widely challenged. Such a shift in the reading curriculum was inevitably opposed by some on ideological as well as educational grounds. Texts (criticised for bad language, immorality or suspect values) became the pretext for a backlash against supposedly progressive teachers for choosing books that encouraged a radical or critical attitude towards society.

During the years of Conservative government, strenuous efforts were made to change this direction of English teaching, first by argument and then by legislation. Right-wing theorists have argued that there is a fixed and authorised English canon that is being ignored in schools. To quote one typical example, in a slim pamphlet Dr John Marenbon constantly returned to what he alleged was 'neglect of the literary heritage in schools' (Marenbon, 1987, p. 28) – indeed he used the word 'heritage' seven times in two pages. His view is that 'children can become good readers . . . only by reading a variety of those works recognised as outstanding by generations of discerning readers' (p. 32). Marenbon repeatedly advocates knowledge of what he calls 'the acknowledged literary masterpieces', as though there is no debate about what these are and as though they will have roughly the same effect on very different readers.

In this situation, how have different versions of the National Curriculum attempted to define what should be read in schools? The members of the Cox Committee expressed their views of suitable reading matter in general terms, concluding that 'it would be wrong to prescribe a list of set texts' (7.14). The report was careful to question oversimple views of the concept of literature and particularly of the 'literary tradition' or 'literary heritage' – terms which it placed in quotation marks (7.14). The NCC's 1993 proposals, however, seemed to assume unquestioningly the notion of 'great literature' and the idea that one can identify 'texts of central importance to our literary heritage'. Consequently the authors were persuaded to suggest particular authors and titles to be studied at different key stages, and these lists were essentially conservative (with a small 'c'). Although the English review group recommended removing the lists, they were later overruled by SCAA, and the 1994 proposals required choices of some poets and novelists (but not dramatists) from given names. It is particularly ironic that this decision should have been made at precisely the same time that the lists of painters and composers in the Art and Music curricula were being eliminated. The uneasy 1995 compromise established a canon of pre-1900 authors of fiction and poetry, but only offers 'examples' of possible twentieth-century writers.

It is unfortunate that the vital issue of what should be read in schools has been narrowed to a confrontational debate about lists of authors. Books must be chosen; writings of the past and the present must be continually evaluated and incorporated into current literary and pedagogical practice. However, who chooses what is to be read and why is a political as well as an educational issue. Strong feelings for or against the 'canon' have given it a symbolic significance. The names on the list are not important in themselves, but for the fact that they are imposed by a quango, with its arbitrary 'before and after 1900' separation of texts (discussed more fully in Judith Atkinson's chapter). If it is sufficient to say that secondary students should read 'drama by major playwrights', then it is hard to see why the same formulation should not be used of other literary forms. English teachers contend that we do not make people literate by insisting that everyone must read the same books. Any arbitrary list *excludes* infinitely more than it includes. There is simply no agreement between authors, teachers, critics and academics about which texts should be 'privileged' by being included. One major objection to defining the literary curriculum in terms of anything resembling set texts is the knock-on effect of *assessing* such a curriculum. English teachers suspect that if students must 'prove their knowledge' of certain works, then they and their teachers will be concerned with those at the expense of 'the habit of reading widely'. In the classroom, there is a huge difference between the imaginative exploration of a Shakespeare play with Year 9 or 10 and preparing the same play for examination or testing. What is testable tends to be low-level explanation and recapitulation, rewarding memory and factual knowledge rather than critical insight and significant personal response to the issues raised in the text (Protherough, 1993). However, from the practical point of view, lists of eighteen novelists and twenty-eight poets published before 1900 can hardly be described as constraining. It would be a rare English department that did not stock and use works by at least some of the suggested writers. The lists can be of some use as illustrative suggestions, providing that the 'set text' associations are contested, that it is acknowledged that the lists were already out of date before they were published, and that there is always a need for them to be challenged, supplemented and updated in any school.

This limiting of debate to the issue of a state-authorised canon has given apparent precedence to texts over readers. It manifests in extreme form a common confusion about the quality of texts and the quality of reading experiences. Whether discussing what should be prescribed or what should be banned, the emphasis is all on the books and not on the way in which those books are received by students. The real issue should be what those readers make of and do with their reading experiences. A great novel can produce a negative response or simple indifference; a 'popular' text can have a significant influence at a particular moment in an individual's development, as many of us can testify. The situation is not helped by the frequent linking of 'undemanding' and 'popular' as though they are necessarily related. Some popular works are actually quite demanding, and it is perfectly possible to skim through major texts in a superficial way that ignores their potential demands (Sarland, 1991). Rather than defining the extension of pupils' reading range in simple terms of 'richer and more demanding *texts*', it would be more helpful to centre on the more sophisticated reading processes involved.

All the proposals insist on the need for adequate resources and a supportive environment to encourage 'wider reading by independent, responsive and enthusiastic readers' (SCAA, 1994, p. 16). Cox was more specific about the provision of 'an environment in which [pupils] are surrounded by books and other reading material presented in an attractive and inviting way'. However, all four versions assume the availability in each English classroom of a wide range of sets of books, magazines, media texts, computer programs and class libraries, supported by a good stock of literature, information and reference books in school libraries (with efficient catalogues or databases). The requirements of Key Stage 3 emphasise a variety of genres (autobiographies, letters, diaries and travel books) as well as a large stock of fiction, poetry and drama, and a huge range of 'information texts in a variety of media'. In this way the National Curriculum gives official support to the widening of subject matter that has been taking place in many English classrooms for a long time. The reality, however, is that few schools are adequately resourced to achieve the aims of the National Curriculum, as was pointed out in the HMI report of 1989. Referring repeatedly to 'limited range', the report concluded that 'if schools are to meet the requirements of the National Curriculum these problems of inadequate and narrow provision will have to be addressed' (HMI, 1989, para 46). In fact, English stocks have continued to run down and book provision has consistently failed to keep pace with inflation in real terms since 1978.

The 1994 proposals for reading show little awareness that the whole concept of 'book culture' is becoming increasingly permeable. Our lives and our environments are shaped by many kinds of stories, some literary but others existing in gossip, films, newspapers, songs, television, video games, and jokes. The very notion of a book as something printed on paper and bound between covers is increasingly becoming outmoded. My grandchildren seem to spend as long listening to audio books as they do turning pages. Electronic texts can be easily stored, printed out in different styles, revised or excerpted, and distributed for reading on screens or on paper. CD-ROM discs enable the reader to support the text with visuals, sound and animation, and to search swiftly for key words and images. Hypertext offers the individual a variety of ways of moving through a text, following up particular interests or seeking help for difficulties that arise. Electronic on-line books (and newspapers in the USA) can link the reader to virtually unlimited resources.

With such changes and the National Curriculum in mind, English departments that are framing their reading policies will need to appraise the general 'literacy environment' of their schools. They might ask, for example, as some have already done:

- How far will students here gain an impression that reading is a source of pleasure, and relevant to all aspects of life?
- Does reading in different modes appear an important activity throughout the school and are reading experiences in different subject areas co-ordinated?
- How are students helped to see the advantages and disadvantages of different ways of encountering texts?
- What attention is given to the making of books, both by the children themselves and through visits by professional authors?
- Will students see their teachers regularly giving time and attention to using and enjoying books and media texts?
- What sort of relationship is established between reading done in school and reading out of school?
- Is publicity for books and media texts widespread throughout the school?
- How effectively are pupils introduced to the library and other sources of reading material and how pleasant are the conditions provided for individual reading in school?

The National Curriculum challenges departments to reassess what is provided for (i) non-literary reading, (ii) individual 'free' reading, (iii) shared reading of the traditional 'English' kind.

### Non-literary reading

The National Curriculum indicates that students should be developing the ability to read different kinds of instructional, study and persuasive texts in a range of media (unattractively presented as 'ability to retrieve and handle information' in the 1994 version). This also involves their capacity for learning across the curriculum (especially in view of the Secretary of State's intention to make teachers of all subjects give attention to the quality of their pupils' English). The particular abilities indicated by the National Curriculum include:

- approaching, to search and to select, to determine function, audience, readability;
- scanning, to gain an overall impression, to assess suitability;
- skimming, to identify where information is located (using indexes, contents lists, chapter heads), to note key points, to answer questions;
- reflecting, to learn or consider, to analyse, to evaluate, to compare.

While English teachers will see the development of these abilities as part of their brief, they will also have to consider the overlap with other subjects, where the National Curriculum requirements for reading are very similar. The chief problem may lie in the need to systematise practice within a school by matching the requisite reading skills to the materials and activities being offered in a range of subjects at different stages. Some of the reading matter, especially newspapers, magazines and pamphlets, will already be available in English stock (though perhaps in need of expanding and bringing up to date) and some can be drawn from other departments or from libraries. However, in view of the detailed prescriptions for literary reading in the 1993 curriculum, it is ironic that what should be read in the area of 'information handling' is left so vague and undefined.

## Individual 'free' reading

Studies indicate the enormous variety within any age range of favourite authors and titles, preferred reading styles, maturity levels and reading abilities. Individual preferences and needs can only be catered for by equally wide-ranging provision. The careful guiding and expanding of such personal reading as envisaged by the National Curriculum depends largely on the skills of teachers:

- discovering more about students' previous reading histories, the sorts of genre they know and like, their principles for choosing texts;
- establishing dialogue with and between pupils about their own choices of reading and the strategies they adopt;
- placing more emphasis on encouraging and monitoring students' own free reading through reading diaries, interviews and other records.

However, it also depends on the conditions established by departmental policy decisions:

- the provision of adequate class libraries (or book boxes where there is no single class base) with multiple copies of a variety of books (so that there can be some sharing of discussion about particular books);
- the continual updating of lists of suggested reading for students, grouped not just by theme or genre but in terms of specific reading demands;
- the agreed allocation of time for pupils to talk or write (in reading journals or elsewhere) about their personal reading;
- the organised provision of 'tasters' (which might sometimes involve video clips) and feedback from students to introduce chosen books more widely;
- a framework for linking stories and poems that are shared by the whole class with a range of possible associated 'free' works;
- the possible temporary reorganising of groups within a year to offer additional choices where funds are limited (opting, for example, for English works coming from one of India, Africa, the Caribbean, or Europe in translation);

- shared responsibilities between colleagues for checking reviews and reading specimen copies of possible new books;
- staff working parties for different age groups to identify gaps in provision for reading, to establish priorities in purchasing and to establish methods for making the best use of resources.

### Shared reading

There are inevitable difficulties at KS3 in selecting texts that will be appropriate for whole-class use, particularly in balancing the different criteria involved. Professional judgements have to weigh up the relative importance of:

- the purposes to be achieved by this reading,
- the literary qualities of the text,
- its likely popularity with students,
- its suitability for the individuals in the group (in terms of difficulty, attitudes conveyed and emotional impact),
- the way in which it relates to the total English programme.

(Protherough, 1983, pp. 146–68)

In planning programmes of shared reading for a group, the National Curriculum proposals do not constrain practices already common in effective English departments. Even the more text-specific versions offer a wide range of choices with no suggestion that all the students in the group must study the same works. The responsibility clearly remains with the department to shape a policy that will establish a coherent structure that students can understand as well as providing necessary individual variety. The sorts of pattern that will underpin development might include the following:

**Clusters** (a short-term form of planning) bring together poems, short stories or novels that are similar in some respect (genre, theme, technique) but where the differences are also significant. Teachers have used, for example, three stories where the narrator proves unreliable, television dramas that make much use of flashback, or four poems using unusual images for everyday objects. Studies suggest that students learn how reading one text alters the way we read another, and how the clustering makes the features and functions of each example stand out, even without specific teaching.

**Sequences** (for long-term planning) are developmentally based, and attempt to place chosen texts in some order of difficulty or complexity. The assumption is that students can successfully approach works that are technically or conceptually demanding if they have previously encountered such features in simpler texts. As one example, a department wishing to exemplify increasingly sophisticated writing about the management of time in fiction could choose a sequence with a single author like Alan Garner (using *The Stone Book* quartet early in secondary school, *The Owl Service* later and *Red Shift* in Year 12) or with several (Penelope Lively, Laurie Lee, Ray Bradbury, D H Lawrence, Emily Bronte, George Eliot and Charles Dickens, say, drawing on the 1994 lists).

**Deliberate repetition** (for either long-term or short-term planning) seeks to challenge the cry of 'We've done it, Miss' by establishing that we have different reading experiences when we return to a text. Students who see no point in reading anything more than once can never have more than a perfunctory response to major works that demand repeated encounters that build on the first. It is intriguing that the National Curriculum does not specifically mention the need for re-reading, although the deepening of reading that comes through 'intertextual' awareness of other books is also provided by remembered previous readings of the same text. Literary education depends on teachers providing occasions for the reappraisal of texts, for acting out the processes of re-reading and for exploring the responses of a group to repeated readings of a text.

## WHAT CONSTITUTES DEVELOPMENT IN READING?

In the National Curriculum, progress is broadly defined in terms of the widening range of texts with which an individual can engage, the increasingly critical awareness of how different kinds of texts 'work' and how they demand distinct reading styles, and the developing ability to express responses and to support judgements. Ultimately, all the versions are grounded in the view that school reading is a kind of ladder climbing, the top of which is defined by what some theoretical 'literate person' or 'skilled adult reader' can do. The great difficulty with this is that there is no clear agreement about just what such a reader's abilities (or 'skills') actually are or how they have come about. Any attempt to describe progress leading towards 'mature' reading behaviour also raises inevitable practical questions. For example:

- Is 'mature' or 'adult' reading necessarily the goal to be achieved?
- How far is it possible objectively to justify any judgement that one response is more 'mature' or 'developed' than another?
- Does the fact that observable changes take place as students grow older necessarily mean that there is a single linear sequence or are there alternative routes?
- If the continuous process is to be divided into separate stages or levels, then are these to be seen as discrete or overlapping?
- Does a model of sequential steps up some normative scale (an assumption

enshrined in the National Curriculum) allow for the variety of recursive learning displayed by real readers?

The Cox Report stressed the idea that developing as a reader means not
only becoming more functionally adept in society but also growing as a
human being: that pupils 'can be helped to develop emotionally, aes-
thetically and intellectually' (16.4). If a reading curriculum is to offer
specific guidance about the range of reading experiences that should be
offered to pupils of different ages and abilities, then it needs to define the
progress by which students learn to become more competent readers.
This will also require some agreed form for recording how that process is
manifested in individual students (discussed later in this chapter). The
original organisation of the National Curriculum, with programmes of
study linked to statements of attainment, was based on assumptions
about progression, but actually offered little help to teachers in the crucial
task of diagnosing where students were located in their progress as
readers. Having to distinguish ten 'levels of attainment' imposed a neatly
sequential view of reading development that was debatable in theory,
inadequately related to real readers in schools and at odds with the
'recursive' view of language learning presented in Cox. The sequences
were frequently dubious and the need to provide bald statements that
distinguished the mandatory ten levels resulted in sets of minor variations on certain vaguely defined terms (insight and view, response and
reaction, explore, explain and demonstrate).

A further difficulty is that statements of attainment in reading are, in
practice, heavily text dependent. To 'justify opinions about a story or
poem, referring to the text' varies in difficulty according to whether the
poem in question is 'Sea Fever', 'The Sick Rose', 'Thrushes' or 'The Waste
Land' (to select from the suggestions listed in the 1993 proposals). It has
been reasonably suggested that an able pupil in primary school would be
able to display all the abilities in reading for information up to level 10
(select and summarise, synthesise, use, evaluate, analyse), assuming that
the books were appropriate for that age. What, in any case, is meant by
'a level 5 reader'? Is there any point in applying the same term to
an enthusiastic primary school reader and a disaffected one at GCSE
stage?

Teachers generally have therefore welcomed the abandonment of detailed statements of attainment in favour of synoptic level descriptions.
They agree with the conclusion that 'the programmes of study . . . should
guide the planning, teaching and day-to-day assessment of pupils' work'
(SCAA, 1994, p. i). It is clear that these formulations need not confine the
teacher or the English department. On the other hand, because of the way
in which they have had to be framed, the level descriptors are heavily
dependent on teacher interpretation, and offer very little practical diag-

nostic help in deciding what stage an individual student has reached or in defining what kinds of development might next be expected. A department's own curriculum should encourage teachers to look more closely at what happens to children reading in their own classrooms as part of their normal work. For example, teachers can consider how individual pupils respond when:

- describing what was happening 'inside their heads' during a shared reading, how they 'realised' the text;
- recording 'where they are' at different points in a narrative;
- annotating an unseen poem;
- framing the reasons for their opinion of a poem or story;
- sharing experiences of books that have been significant for them;
- explaining what books they return to more than once, and why;
- asked to formulate on paper their first responses to a poem or story in preparation for a class discussion;
- invited to raise their own questions about the text read.

Without any need for artificial testing, it should then be possible to form a clearer impression of:

- How children of different levels of ability actually read.
- What seems to mark off those considered as 'good' readers, and how we decide what 'good' means.
- What sorts of pleasure children derive from different kinds of reading matter at different stages of development.
- The differences which gender and cultural background seem to make in the ways that certain texts are read.
- The influence of 'free' reading on shared reading in school.

Teachers who have been looking in this way for signs of development in the reading abilities of their children, and relating small-scale studies to the tentative models that have been advanced, will be anxious to supplement any National Curriculum model with some mapping of more specific markers of development. This will ideally involve building up over the years a set of exemplar material that will make real the different ways in which items like 'write a critical and appreciative response to a text' may be understood at different developmental stages. The bald statements 'support their views' (level 5) or 'justifying their views' (level 6) need to be grounded in more specific markers of the increasing ability to explore preferences in talking or writing about literary works, moving from simple 'liking' to reasoned 'judging'. It is possible to chart students' 'progress' from assuming the rightness of their own immediate reactions (and reluctance to accept that others may have different views) as manifested in abilities like the following:

- seeking for some justification (a particular theme, quality or effect) as a reason for liking or disliking a text;
- displaying willingness to entertain judgements that differ from their own; showing interest in comparing reasons for preferences;
- realising the distinction between judgements about the experience of reading and those about the text;
- drawing together different elements of response to create an overall reading;
- attempting to sustain judgements by reference to critical considerations (credibility, structure, vividness, characterisation, etc.);
- supporting judgement by describing the importance of the work in terms either of general meaning or of personal significance;
- showing increased willingness to generalise, to compare one text with another;
- understanding that there are no final judgements and that we all remake our interpretations and evaluations.

Taking the reading of fiction as one example, members of an English department might work together to develop sets of indicators like the two examples that follow.

## WIDENING UNDERSTANDING OF THE VARIETIES OF NARRATIVE STRUCTURE, INCLUDING THE NON-CHRONOLOGICAL (FROM SIMPLE FLASHBACK TO MORE COMPLEX REORDERING OF THE TIME SCHEME)

Students seem to progress from an unreflective interest in action, expecting to be carried along by the story and impatient with anything that holds up the action, to:

- predict what is likely to happen next in a narrative; suggest probable endings appropriate to the genre, and enjoy texts that challenge such expectations; supply potential completions to an 'open' ending;
- be aware that narrative is more than action; fill in gaps in the text and frame expectations about characters and the way that they might behave;
- consider 'what if . . . ?' (other ways in which the narrative might have developed), and hypothesise about what characters might be doing when absent from the page or off the stage;
- recognise some of the deliberate effects created by the author (e.g. in setting, pace, dialogue) and explain what they contribute to the narrative;
- understand the way in which the narrative exists in relationship to others, and how reading is affected by this understanding;

- understand (and possibly question) the ideology of the text, relating it to the reader's own experience, situation and personality.

## AWARENESS OF THE SIGNIFICANCE OF THE VIEWPOINT(S) FROM WHICH A STORY IS TOLD, AND ABILITY TO DISTINGUISH THE VOICES OF NARRATOR AND CHARACTERS

Students progress from reading a text unquestioningly as a direct representation of some 'reality', to reveal such abilities as:

- distinguishing between texts told by an impersonal, 'omniscient' narrator and those told through the voice of a character;
- retelling events from the viewpoint of another character involved;
- suggesting the ways that one character might view others, their behaviour and motivation;
- showing awareness that a narrator is selective and can be unreliable;
- detecting shifts of 'voice' within a work;
- realising that the 'persona' of the implied narrator is not necessarily identical with that of the author;
- responding to a work without necessarily accepting the viewpoint, judgements and attitudes of the story-teller;
- responding to the interplay of the author's voice with those voices attributed to different characters;
- distinguishing perceptual (who sees?) and conceptual (who judges?) points of view;
- being aware of irony and indications of self-deception.

Monitoring the work of students against specific criteria in this way inevitably involves record-keeping. Certainly in the past, the failure to understand how children developed as readers and the failure to keep adequate records of how and what they read went hand in hand. A pervasive vagueness about just what progress meant transmitted itself from teachers to pupils. The Senior Chief Inspector wrote in his annual report for 1990–1 that 'many pupils were not being given a sufficiently clear idea of their progress or any indication of how they might improve the quality of their work' (HMI, 1992, para 62). Schools have already discovered that the National Curriculum has intensified the desire for better management of the transition from primary to secondary. Secondary teachers are still hammering out a policy for using primary records (Who has access to them? How can they best be used? How can the secondary English department build on them?) and for their own record-keeping.

One useful format, developed with variations in a number of schools, is the portfolio, built up over the years. As far as reading is concerned this might include:

from the pupils –

- accounts of their own earlier reading history,
- indications of their likes and dislikes,
- lists of books enjoyed during the year,
- reading logs or diaries,
- self-assessment comments on progress noted in themselves and changes in response during the year;

from the teachers –

- brief records of the tasks completed by the student,
- indication of reading abilities developed during the year,
- record of discussions with the student about reading and associated work,
- representative samples of student work,
- details of any more formal tests or examinations,
- observations and recommendations for future development;

from parents –

- observations about children's home reading and preferences,
- comments on the evolving records.

The teachers' comments will be related (but not confined) to the statements of attainment, and should not be simply of a list-ticking kind. Unlike 'standardised' reading tests, which are wholly impersonal, the records implied by the National Curriculum are personal. A teacher's observations of what children do and say as they read and reflect on their reading are inevitably selective; those observations are interpreted and categorised, to consider diagnostically where the individual is and might be going (Leach and McGregor, 1992).


## CONCLUSION

For years there has been much hypocritical panic about reading 'standards' or the reading habits of young people and much of that panic has been ideologically motivated. Will a reading curriculum help to allay any of those fears?

At the time of writing, it is no wonder that English teachers are confused after being presented with so much conflicting 'official' advice. In general, they felt that the Cox proposals had the potential to improve work in schools and were much less enthusiastic about the 1993 NCC revisions (significantly presented as the work of the council, and not its English committee). The SCAA document may say that its 'concern is to encourage pupils to be independent, responsive and enthusiastic readers' (SCAA, 1994, p. iv) but clearly only teachers and students can realise that concern. In the long run, any national curriculum is simply posturing unless it carries English teachers with it. The ultimate test of any curriculum is what it does for the students who follow it. If publishing a national reading curriculum is to have any beneficial effect, then – as this chapter has argued – it depends on giving teachers adequate time and resources to organise individual reading programmes for their own schools and to improve their methods of monitoring and recording pupils' progress. Sir Ron Dearing has made it clear that this is unlikely to happen if the government continues to make time-consuming demands for reporting that progress and simultaneously imposes simplistic national tests. The time and resources being wasted would be better devoted to in-service work with teachers and to putting more books on the shelves.

## REFERENCES AND FURTHER READING

DES (1989) *English for Ages 5 to 16*, HMSO
DFE (1993) *English for Ages 5 to 16*, HMSO
DFE (1995) *English in the National Curriculum*, HMSO
HMI (1989) *Reading Policy and Practice at Ages 5–14*, DES
HMI (1992) *Education in England, 1990–1*, DES
Leach, Jenny and McGregor, Val (1992) 'Making the transition: towards a secondary language record', *The English & Media Magazine*, Spring 1992, pp. 27–31
Marenbon, John (1987) *English, Our English*, Centre for Policy Studies, London
Protherough, Robert (1983) *Developing Response to Fiction*, Open University Press, Milton Keynes
Protherough, Robert (1986) *Teaching Literature for Examinations*, Open University Press, Milton Keynes
Protherough, Robert (1989) *Students of English*, Routledge, London
Protherough, Robert (1993) 'More absurd than in other subjects?', *English in Education*, Vol. 27, No. 1, pp. 10–18
Sarland, Charles (1991) *Young People Reading: Culture and Response*, Open University Press, Milton Keynes
SCAA (1994) *English in the National Curriculum: Draft Proposals (May 1994)*, Schools Curriculum & Assessment Authority
Scottish Education Department (1990) *Working Paper 2 English Language 5–14*, SED, Edinburgh

# Chapter 4

# How do we teach pre-twentieth-century literature?

*Judith Atkinson*

Wall displays of 'The Rime of the Ancient Mariner' retold as comic strip by 12-year-olds; a girl choosing Clare's poem 'First Love' as her favourite from her own anthology of love poetry; life in Miss Havisham's gloomy house described in Estella's words by a 14-year-old; Blake's 'A Poison Tree' discussed with absorption by four 11-year-olds. . . . These are snapshots of pupils working with literature written before the twentieth century; work done in classrooms before the National Curriculum was even mooted. So what is new in the gentle suggestion in Cox that the range of literature presented to pupils should include 'some works written before the twentieth century' or in the fiercer directive from the revised Orders that at Key Stages 3 and 4 pupils 'should read' works written or published 'before 1900'? The difference for many engaged in English teaching lies in the word 'should'. The teacher who read Coleridge's poem to a Year 8 class *chose* to do so for a cluster of different reasons: she felt confident after previous experience with this and other classes that the pupils would be gripped by the story and that many would enjoy it; she wanted to make links both with other literature the class had met and with the work they had been doing on sounds and colour in poetry; she knew from her familiarity with the needs and development of individuals and of the group as a whole that they were ready for the poem and, finally, she was following departmental policy in planning to introduce non-contemporary poetry as part of her year's work with the class.

For such a teacher there are several areas of concern when she considers how the National Curriculum is already changing her practice in working on literature with children, and threatening to affect it even more radically.

• It seems from the 1994 review that she may be losing responsibility for planning her own programmes of work. The directives seem to express a lack of trust in her experience and ability to plan a reading programme for particular pupils, classes and situations. They are threatening because with their prescriptions for particular authors for particular age groups they appear to take away the English teacher's cherished freedom to choose texts to meet the needs and interests of known pupils.

- She will be uncomfortably aware that decisions about her teaching of literature are being made by politicians or political appointees rather than by fellow professionals whose ideas, she knows, arise from experience with children and classrooms. Various National Curriculum documents show that these politicians have created a climate in which the key to the raising of standards is seen to be through the content rather than the processes of learning. In this context English is a misfit and the documents have striven to give 'rigour' to the subject by stressing knowledge of and about literature. Pupils who know the difference between similes and metaphors and can recognise that a poem is by Wordsworth have clearly learnt something; they also have knowledge which can be readily tested.

- As she reads newspapers and watches television she will realise that politicians and the media have combined to support the move to greater 'rigour' by creating a picture of generations of pupils who have been denied their 'literary heritage' and have instead been brought up on a diet of twentieth-century literature and media texts. Both the Secretary of State for Education and the Prime Minister chose to highlight this in their speeches to the Conservative Party Conference in 1992.

> Of course it's hard for parents to have much confidence in exam boards when some of them include television programmes such as 'Neighbours' and even 'Allo Allo' in their English syllabuses.
>
> (John Patten, 7 October 1992)

> English exams should be about Literature, not soap opera. And I promise you this: there'll be no GCSE in 'Eldorado' – even supposing someone is still watching it.
>
> (John Major, October 1992)

The teacher, knowing that she and her colleagues work with a balance of 'classic' and contemporary texts, will recognise this picture as a parody of what actually goes on in English classrooms. She may, however, agree with Graham Frater HMI, the former staff inspector for English, that enthusiasm for excellent contemporary texts has disturbed that balance:

> evidence tends to show that relatively little pre-twentieth-century literature is handled before GCSE and much of what is handled tends to be poetry. What I think you've got to judge is whether that is appropriate or not . . .
>
> (Ogborn and Simons, 1993)

Even so she may feel that to prescribe particular pre-twentieth-century authors is the wrong way to encourage teachers to extend the reading programme for their pupils.

- As she herself feels comfortable with her department's mix of contemporary and 'classic' literature she feels uneasy about the way in which the National Curriculum documents and, more particularly, both the Revised Order and the Dearing Review, privilege pre-twentieth-century literature. With their reiteration of the concept of 'our literary heritage' (explored in more detail in chapter 3) they create unreal distinctions between the texts pupils will meet. Placed in a special 'elite' category in this way pre-twentieth-century texts either create false expectations in teachers and pupils, or seem in anticipation to present problems for reading and understanding.

- As a reader inspired by exciting and often subversive non-contemporary authors from different countries, she feels ill at ease with claims made for the superiority of all things English, including its literature. She will see that it is no coincidence that such claims are made during a period of widespread uncertainty about England's place in the world, represented on the one hand by articles in the liberal press analysing the situation:

> Our streets are no longer safe, we're giving up power to Brussels, we can't even win at cricket any more. Whatever happened to the English?
>
> *(Guardian*, 28 July 1993)

and on the other by assertions of the value of English institutions which are seen to enshrine the country's greatness:

> the long shadows falling across the country ground, the warm beer, the invincible green suburbs, dog lovers and pools fillers . . . old maids bicycling to Holy Communion through the morning mist.
>
> (John Major in a speech to a Conservative Party European Group, April 1993)

One of these institutions, publicly invoked by both the Prime Minister and the Heir Apparent, is English Literature. For the teacher the tough social criticism of Dickens or the subversive ironies of Kipling's Indian stories have little to do with the notion of 'Englishness' expressed by the Prime Minister or by the authors of the Revised Order. Nor is she comfortable with a nostalgic concept of Englishness which is irrelevant both to contemporary adolescents and to the classrooms where many different languages and cultures are represented.

So where does the present situation leave this English teacher faced with implementing a national curriculum and wondering how to approach pre-twentieth-century literature? The first point to make to her is that when there is so much disagreement about what is to be read in school (as Robert Protherough discusses in chapter 3) the disparity between views can be an ally rather than an enemy. In the end when others disagree it is the individual teacher and department's responsibility to decide how their reading programmes will be balanced and how such texts will be taught. It is also important for the teacher to ignore the rhetoric which surrounds this issue and to recognise that this is not a reintroduction of 'the classics' into English classrooms but a consolidation of what already takes place. Viewed in this way the highlighting of pre-twentieth-century literature is a reminder to her and to other English teachers to rediscover the pleasures of such texts and to consider how to adapt existing good practice to introduce them to young readers.

## MAKING DECISIONS ABOUT BOOKS

It is possible in the face of the lists of authors presented in recent curriculum documents to feel that teachers are no longer free to make their own decisions about the books they wish to share with their classes. However, unlike an examination board's list of mandatory set texts, this list is a starting point for departments and individual teachers to use for their own discussions about book choices. Here are some of the considerations for taking into account during such discussions:

- In choosing pre-twentieth-century texts to work on with classes the same principles apply as for more familiar contemporary texts. Teachers need to ask themselves questions such as: how will this text serve my overall programme for this class? why this particular book? what are the chief merits of the text that I shall hope to help pupils respond to? will there be characters or situations which will interest pupils? will they enjoy the text? will there be opportunities for individual readers to identify with situations and issues? what particular difficulties may have to be overcome?
- It is important to remember that the list of authors from which choices are to be made covers both Key Stages 3 and 4, making possible the 'flexibility' promised in the 1994 Review's Commentary. Equally, although the review is specific about the number of poets and writers of fiction pupils 'should' encounter at each key stage, it is not specific about how these works should be read and in what context; there is no requirement for a writer's work to be 'studied'. What follows from this is the importance of long-term planning to ensure a balance between texts from different periods, with a conscious intention to make links between them: e.g. a small selection of Clare's poems about animals

could be set alongside Hughes' in the spirit of influential anthologies like Penguin's *Voices*. Planning of this kind is described in more detail in chapter 3.

- One of the disadvantages of the high-profile debate about pre-twentieth-century literature has been its effect on teachers', parents' and perhaps pupils' perceptions of such texts. There has been a tendency to view, for example, Tennyson's poems with either reverence or suspicion, forgetting that many of these poems are more immediately readable than the sometimes allusive contemporary poetry often presented to children. The whole concept of 'pre-twentieth-century literature' risks creating a ghetto of texts which are seen to be different in a variety of ways. In choosing books for classes it is important to 'demystify' earlier authors, and, for example, to recognise and highlight for pupils the subversive nature of *Huckleberry Finn* or *Treasure Island* or to place books from different periods but the same genre side by side, *Tom Sawyer* alongside *Tyke Tiler*, for example.
- Departments which have made careful and conscious decisions to buy in a stock which represents a balance of female and male authors, of different cultures and, in fiction, of different kinds of leading characters may feel that the balance is threatened by the addition of more pre-twentieth-century texts. It will certainly be important when discussing choices to argue for the inclusion of sometimes neglected women writers like Emily Dickinson or Mary Shelley; to look carefully at the presentation of race in *Huckleberry Finn*, *Robinson Crusoe* or the Indian stories of Rudyard Kipling; to bear in mind spirited heroines like Kate Hardcastle in *She Stoops to Conquer*, Catherine Morland in *Northanger Abbey* or Bathsheba Everdene in *Far from the Madding Crowd*; and to prepare to confront the issue that, unlike most contemporary writers for young people, an author like Stevenson was consciously writing for boy readers.
- Choosing texts for whole-class use, particularly in Year 9 at Key Stage 3 and for mixed ability groups, is always difficult. Pre-twentieth-century texts appear to pose an additional problem in the reading demands they might make on pupils unfamiliar with some of the language and references. In considering such texts for whole-class use it is worth remembering that some contemporary texts teachers would not hesitate to use make comparable demands on young readers. Teachers should also be encouraged by their own successful experiences of introducing Shakespeare to younger pupils, often in mixed-ability groups, when effective teaching approaches demonstrate that unfamiliar language and references are less of a barrier to enjoyment and understanding than might be imagined.
- Chapter 3 has already considered the importance of adequate funding

for the kind of reading programme put forward by the National Curriculum documents. In relation to pre-twentieth-century texts there might be a temptation for hard-pressed departments to fall back on whatever dusty sets of books are still in the stockroom, but decisions about choices should not be at the mercy of such considerations. At the moment attractive paper-backed editions of 'the classics' are widely and, more importantly, cheaply available. Alternatively, as books written before 1900 are out of copyright it should be possible in schools with the right equipment to print out copies from disc cheaply and to provide pupils with texts they can work on and with.

As a starting point for departmental discussion of book choices for whole-class use here is a list of *suggested* allocations of texts to year groups. Works by listed authors have been included, but alongside some perhaps less familiar writers.

**Year 7**

*Stories*

*Treasure Island; Tom Sawyer; A Christmas Carol; Beowulf;* different versions of myths and legends, e.g. by Ian Seraillier, Leon Garfield and Edward Blishen, Kevin Crossley-Holland; *Sir Gawain and the Green Knight* in a modern version by Ian Seraillier.

*Poems*

Clare – animal and seasons poems; Blake – 'Lamb' and 'Tyger'; Wordsworth – skating episode from *The Prelude*; 'Christopher Smart Considers his Cat, Jeoffry'.

**Year 8**

*Novels and short stories*

Sherlock Holmes stories; *Tom Brown's Schooldays; Huckleberry Finn;* the early part of *David Copperfield; Robinson Crusoe.*

*Poems*

Tennyson – 'The Lady of Shallott'; Keats – 'La Belle Dame Sans Merci'; Coleridge – 'The Rime of the Ancient Mariner', 'Kubla Khan'.

**Year 9**

*Plays*

*She Stoops to Conquer.*

*Novels and short stories*

*Oliver Twist; Northanger Abbey;* some of Rudyard Kipling's *Plain Tales from the Hills;* the first two books from *Gulliver's Travels;* short stories by Thomas Hardy.

*Poems*

'Prologue' and some stories from *The Canterbury Tales;* Blake – 'A Poison Tree', 'The Sick Rose', 'Holy Thursday' poems, 'The Chimney Sweeper', 'London'; selections from Emily Dickinson; Tennyson – 'The Lotos Eaters', 'Ulysses', 'The Charge of the Light Brigade'; Wordsworth – 'Daffodils' and other poems set alongside Dorothy Wordsworth's *Journal.*

**Years 10 and 11**

*Plays*

*The Importance of Being Earnest; School for Scandal; The Rivals.*

*Novels*

*A Tale of Two Cities; Great Expectations; Far from the Madding Crowd; The Mayor of Casterbridge; Frankenstein; Jane Eyre; Pride and Prejudice; Mary Barton.*

*Poems*

Browning – 'My Last Duchess', 'Porphyria's Lover'; Keats – 'Ode to Autumn' and 'Ode to a Nightingale'; Shakespeare – a selection from the *Sonnets;* Clare – 'First Love', 'I Am'; Marvell – 'To His Coy Mistress'; Arnold – 'Dover Beach'.

## APPROACHES TO TEACHING

Many older, and some younger, English teachers may have memories of their own school lessons passed in a daze of boredom as *Cranford* was read haltingly around the class. They may remember homeworks spent in writing chapter summaries of *Northanger Abbey*. There is no reason why 'academic' approaches like these should be considered more applicable to pre-twentieth-century texts than to contemporary literature, even when such texts are being 'studied' for examinations – yet they often are. The same teachers may equally recall occasions when they were held by a teacher's reading aloud of 'Kubla Khan' or 'The Lotos Eaters', or became involved in the characters and dilemmas of apparently simple myths through creating Theseus's version of the killing of the Minotaur. Such approaches, designed to arouse and sustain interest and involvement, would be common good practice in classrooms where contemporary literature is being taught and they are equally effective and productive for earlier texts. Detailed discussion and description of such approaches can be found elsewhere, but to consider their application to pre-twentieth-century texts a teacher might ask the following questions:

- What should I do to prepare for reading this text?
- How will the text be read?
- What activities should I prepare for pupils to help them to respond to the text during their reading?
- What activities will help pupils to come to terms with the text and to express their responses after reading?

## PREPARING TO READ

Although the best way to bring a text to a group of pupils may sometimes be to begin reading without any preliminaries, many are more effectively introduced with activities which prepare for the first experience of reading. This is particularly true of non-contemporary texts in which language, setting and ideas may be alien to young readers. Some of the aims of such activities will be: to arouse thought and reaction to some of the issues the book will provoke; to introduce situations and dilemmas characters will meet; to prepare imaginatively for an unusual or un-familiar setting; to introduce a new genre or to make links with genres a class has already met. The word 'activity' has been carefully chosen. To *inform* pupils about the historical context of a book, or about the bi-ography of its author, is not to prepare them for the experience of reading. The activities teachers devise should bring into play the faculties of imagination, emotion and thought which will later make up the active process of reading. It may later enhance a young reader's enjoyment of *David Copperfield* to discover that some of the early scenes of the novel are autobiographical, but knowledge of this kind is alien to the imaginative world a writer first presents to a new reader. What follows are some suggestions of activities for whole-class use:

## INTRODUCING THEMES

- Using improvisation perhaps followed by discussion: e.g. a modern Scrooge confronted with examples of contemporary commercialised Christmas; scenes of exaggerated 'Gothic' horror set alongside deflating reality to prepare for *Northanger Abbey*; rival groups plotting to uncover a cache of ill-gotten treasure and then arguing the case for the rightful owner, as in *Treasure Island*.
- Using other reading: e.g. a story from *Stories from Black History* by Julius Lester before *Huckleberry Finn*; a collage of extracts from contemporary journalism and Mayhew's Journals before *Oliver Twist*.
- Using pupils' own writing: e.g. desert island survival story before *Robinson Crusoe*; visual and aural observation of nature before Clare or Wordsworth.

## INTRODUCING CHARACTERS AND SITUATIONS

- Using improvisation perhaps followed by 'hot-seating': e.g. different groups improvising and showing different situations involved in *She Stoops to Conquer*, i.e. Hardcastle parents, doting mother and impossible son, usually confident man transformed by shyness with women, a girl in disguise; a Bathsheba Everdene in a contemporary situation having to choose between three contrasting men.
- Using pupils' own writing: e.g. to write a chilling opener for a novel, given the 'ingredients' of the opening of *Great Expectations*; to create a set of contemporary characters setting out on a coach trip holiday and to write the introductory portraits before Chaucer's 'Prologue'.

## INTRODUCING SETTINGS

- Using visual stimuli to prepare for unfamiliar costumes, buildings or landscapes when these are important to first responses to a text: e.g. medieval drawings etc. before the 'Prologue'; early photographs of Victorian rural workers (as, for example, in *A Country Camera 1844– 1914* by Gordon Winter, Penguin, 1973) before work by Hardy.

## INTRODUCING GENRE

- Using other media: e.g. short TV clips of contemporary fictional detective pairings before Sherlock Holmes; extracts from Alan Bennett's 'Talking Heads' before Browning monologues.
- Using other reading: e.g. excerpts from varieties of twentieth-century school story before *Tom Brown*; excerpts from various retellings of the King Arthur stories before Tennyson.

- Using pupils' own writing: e.g. image chains before Blake's 'Poison Tree', or Emily Dickinson's 'It Sifts from Leaden Sieves'.

Missing from this list are video recordings of TV or film adaptations of pre-twentieth-century novels. There is clearly much that pupils can gain from watching either extracts or whole versions of such adaptations; the question that needs considering is *when* this experience is most useful. Watching before meeting the text could help pupils to visualise settings and gain a sense of the atmosphere of a book; it could also generate involvement and enthusiasm. Equally it could impose another reader's (the director's) view of characters and situations on pupils before their initial meeting with the text. Alternatively, watching recordings after reading could provide opportunities to discuss adaptation and other readers' interpretations. Teachers need to make their own decisions about when to introduce such recordings in the light of the features particular to the text or adaptation or class.

## READING THE TEXT

When books are being shared with a whole class, particularly when pupils with a wide range of abilities are together, the mechanics of reading texts, and novels in particular, often pose a problem. This could be especially true with pre-twentieth-century texts which challenge pupils through their length, pace and narrative complexity, their language and their often alien references. The one clear principle which should underlie any teacher's planning is that any method chosen needs to arouse and sustain pupils' interest, promote their enjoyment and enhance their understanding. To be avoided are unprepared reading round the class of an uncut text and unguided independent reading for homework. Instead, these are suggested ways of meeting the challenges posed by non-contemporary texts.

## THE LENGTH, PACE AND COMPLEXITY OF NOVELS

If a novel is to be a shared reading experience substantial parts of the text will be read out loud in the classroom. Most contemporary books written for young people and some adult novels, such as *Of Mice and Men*, are short enough for the whole text to be read in instalments with breaks for activities for sharing responses. Despite their brevity, though, some benefit from thoughtful cutting when, for example, overlong description or explanation holds up the narrative momentum. Nineteenth-century novels are frequently longer, move at a more leisurely pace and, particularly in the case of works by Dickens, keep several interconnected plots and groups of characters in play at the same time. Carefully planned cutting is essential if pupils' interest is to be held through the narrative. A first step in the preparation stage is to divide the novel up into 'phases' – the writers themselves often help here as many of their stories are already presented in instalments or books. A decision then needs to be made about which passages in each phase are important for the narrative and have either particular potential for being read out loud or aspects which will be valuable for pupils to work on. These will be the passages for sharing in class. It may sometimes work to a book's advantage to cut explanatory opening passages, or, alternatively, a class's interest can be caught and points later explored about narrative shape if the reading of a novel is begun with a dramatic or climactic episode from later in the book. Pupils can then explore theories about how that point in the story was reached before returning to earlier scenes.

When the chosen episodes form the shared reading experience in the classroom, to keep the thread of the story going and to provide for the variety of reading abilities represented in any classroom, the linking narrative passages need to be 'covered'. If the teacher's aim is to move forward quite swiftly through a less important phase of a book, pupils can be given the choice to read on for themselves to a given point and the teacher can introduce the next shared reading lesson with a résumé. When the passage to be missed is more interesting or contentious, home-works can be set for different groups within the class: for those who would find unaided reading difficult, activities to consolidate work on the novel so far, for example a contribution to a time-line wallchart or to a class comic-strip version of the book, and for those able or keen to read on, a task to report back in some way to the rest of the class about the intervening narrative. Despite the length of many such novels it is important to keep up the pace of the class's collective reading. Even a class which has been fired with enthusiasm at their first encounter with a novel will be unable to sustain that interest if the reading of the book stretches in a leisurely way over several weeks. This does mean that in preparing a block of work centred on a shared novel the timing has to be carefully worked out.

## THE CHALLENGE OF THE LANGUAGE

Contemporary pupils are versatile language users who think nothing of adapting to American or Australian idioms when they watch television. Pre-twentieth-century English can be as accessible if reading is approached with confidence. If the teacher reads aloud with panache, obviously relishing, for example, Dickens's descriptions of characters or the exotic language of 'Kubla Khan', and that reading is supplemented with, for example, extracts from taped versions, pupils will be encouraged to try for themselves. The teacher can then share the reading with pupils who either have prepared extracts or take parts in the dialogue. Prepared poetry performances or poetry programmes taped by groups also give pupils the chance to rehearse and then enjoy reading previously unfamiliar texts aloud. There are few passages in contemporary texts which can give as much pleasure in being read aloud as 'The Rime of the Ancient Mariner', or the arrival of Blind Pew, or Clare's 'Badger', or Wordsworth's description of skating, or the opening of *Great Expectations*, or Blake's 'Tyger'.

## UNFAMILIAR REFERENCES

Pupils, particularly conscientious ones, can nag both themselves and the teacher if there are references in the text that they fail to understand. The important thing to remember, and then to communicate to pupils, is how we read ourselves. In reading for the essence of meaning and for enjoyment most adult readers pass over unfamiliar references, unless they hold up understanding or are intriguing for other reasons. The same principle should apply in the classroom. Reading out loud which is intended to promote enjoyment should not be interrupted by textual explanation. If in preparing a passage beforehand the teacher feels that explanation is necessary for meaning this should be done before reading and if possible through a modern analogy, for example a contemporary comparison to throw light on the Hardcastles' views of fashion in *She Stoops to Conquer*.

## EXPLORING RESPONSES DURING READING

Departments and individual teachers will be familiar with the wide range of activities which can be devised to promote pupils' responses after or during first encounters with texts. They are perhaps even more important for use with pre-twentieth-century texts when pupils may need encouragement and support, particularly from each other. These are just a few familiar activities with suggestions of how they might be applied. Teachers will need to make their own decisions about how a sequence of such activities will be built up and also about the purposes the activities will serve for that particular text and group of pupils.

## INDIVIDUAL ACTIVITIES

- Reading journals or commentaries on tape through which pupils can record immediate and considered reactions, ask teachers or partners questions, make links with their own experiences etc.

- Picturing: jotting down immediate visual responses to 'open' poems like those of Blake, Emily Dickinson or Coleridge; making informal or worked-on illustrations of scenes from novels, e.g. Marley's ghost, Canterbury pilgrims from their portraits; creating staging and costume designs for plays.
- Writing, to promote returning to parts of the text in order to consider them from different perspectives: to look at characters from a different viewpoint, interviews with other characters, e.g. Joe, Biddy, Miss Havisham and Estella for their opinions of Pip at different points in the narrative; to realise some of the effects of first-person narration, to transpose a scene into the words of another character or into another medium, e.g. Jane Eyre's first meeting with Mr Rochester in his words or as a scene from a radio adaptation; to look at alternative interpretations of events in novels, to construct two different accounts of the same scene, e.g. conflicting newspaper accounts of the rival celebrations organised in Casterbridge by Henchard and Farfrae.

## GROUP ACTIVITIES

- Prediction: groups using textual clues to make predictions about plot, character development or the resolution of issues, e.g. where has Pip's money come from? what will happen at the end of Kipling's story 'Beyond the Pale'? how will the complications in *She Stoops to Conquer* be worked out?
- Hot-seating to explore presentation of character: e.g. Browning's Duke about his last Duchess; the crew of the Hispaniola about their motives for going to Treasure Island.
- Cloze activities: for work on word choice, imagery, rhyme and rhythm.
- Adaptations of parts of texts into other media: in order to consider narrative shape, the use of narration, dialogue, etc.
- Discussion of others' adaptations of scenes from novels or plays after watching extracts from film or television versions.
- Discussion, either informal or as debate or mock trial: to exchange ideas about interpretations, to consider issues raised by the text, e.g. Silas Marner's actions, Henchard's treatment of Elizabeth Jane.
- Preparing explanatory presentations for the rest of the class: to give a purposeful forum for discussion of meaning and how interpretation can be conveyed to others.
- Work on performing scenes from plays with an emphasis on trying different styles, e.g. experimenting with the timing of the Gwendolyn/ Cecily scene, or the playing of farce in *She Stoops to Conquer*.

During Key Stage 4 when a pre-twentieth-century text may need to be studied more intensively for a terminal examination it is still preferable to plan a sequence of activities of this kind during the reading of the text than to set pupils scene or chapter summaries. When there are the twin needs to respond thoughtfully and to assimilate a text, methods which promote understanding in a memorable way will prove more effective than note-taking which often only deals with plot. Reading journals can be used to record what pupils have discovered through individual or shared activities. The teacher's role during this phase of work with a text is primarily to structure activities so that pupils' involvement will be sustained and their responses drawn out and heightened, particularly from sharing their ideas with others. Careful thought needs to be given to the framing of activities and to the wording of questions, instructions and guidance.

## ACTIVITIES AFTER READING

A class of 14-year-olds who after reading *Oliver Twist* are given the assignment 'Show Dickens's power as a story-teller through looking at the narrative, characterisation and dialogue in *Oliver Twist*' will understandably feel both baffled and disappointed. After enjoying the novel pupils will feel that this is a 'boring' task but they will also feel unequal to it. The title of the assignment with its abstract concepts, terms with which they may not be familiar and its generalised invitation is inappropriate for pupils of their age and development. Yet the teacher who set the assignment felt that this was an appropriate way to ask young readers to respond to Dickens, although assignments previously set on *Z for Zachariah* had included a diary, an alternative ending and a comparison between the two central characters. Making such a distinction between texts from different periods perhaps expresses teachers' reverence for 'the classics', or a feeling that they are expected to treat such texts differently. Whatever the reason, the distinction is a false one. The criteria for framing activities and writing assignments which will crystallise and express response to a text are the same for a novel by Robert O'Brien as they are for one by Charles Dickens. They should be directed to draw out pupils' understanding of the particular aspects for which the text has been chosen, framed and written in terms accessible to the age group and offering pupils at different stages of development within a class the chance to explore and demonstrate their understanding. Alongside more familiar individual assignments, it is important to continue to plan group activities through which pupils return collaboratively to the text to re-read and rethink.

The following activities, familiar to most teachers from their work with contemporary books, are listed here with suggestions for application to pre-twentieth-century texts.

## NOVELS AND PLAYS

### Group activities

- Performing the trial of a character, to consider motives, relationships, differing viewpoints: Elizabeth Jane, Farfrae, citizens of Casterbridge for the death of Henchard; Scrooge for his meanness.
- Taping or performing a radio/TV interview programme, to explore character, character development, relationships: Pip after the events of the novel; the crew returned from Treasure Island; Huck Finn about his adventures and meetings with other characters.
- Dramatisation of a sequence of scenes, to examine the roles of dialogue and narrative in story-telling and to consider the narrative viewpoint: scenes from *Treasure Island*, *Jane Eyre*.
- Working to produce plans for film adaptation of a story or novel, to consider and discuss the text as a whole, e.g. storyboard, sample dialogue, character portraits, setting and costume, selling angle. Where possible to follow this up with watching a film version, e.g. David Lean's *Great Expectations*.
- Through wall display or oral presentation to introduce the text to new readers, e.g. parents, another class.

### Individual activities

#### Looking at characterisation

- Portraits of a central figure in the words of two or three other characters, to realise viewpoints, ironies, etc.: Long John Silver as seen by different members of the *Hispaniola* crew; Mr Micawber as seen by David, his wife and a debt collector.
- Diaries or letters to explore characters' feelings, thoughts and development: Biddy at different stages in her relationship with Pip; Marlowe's diary before, during and after his stay with the Hardcastles.
- Explaining the importance of scenes which cast light on characters and their development: Pip with Joe Gargery – in the forge, on Joe's first London visit and during Pip's illness; Catherine Morland with Isabella in the Bath Assembly Rooms and during her night of discoveries in Northanger Abbey.
- Exploring comparisons and contrasts between characters: Catherine and Isabella; Mr Rochester and St John Rivers.

#### Looking at plot and narration

- Rewriting endings, to consider author's choices, build on narrative clues, etc.: a possible third ending to *Great Expectations*.

- Writing extra scenes which the author chose to omit, to consider narrative shape: Troy's first meeting with Fanny Robin; Estella and Miss Havisham discussing Pip after his first visit.
- Creating a schematic diagram of a complex plot, to explore the mechanics of plot-making: *The Mayor of Casterbridge*; *Oliver Twist*.

### Looking at setting

- Writing impressionistically to convey the setting and atmosphere of places important to a novel: Paris and London from *A Tale of Two Cities*; the river from *Huckleberry Finn*.
- Explaining the importance of different settings to a novel: of Jane Eyre's different homes; of the workhouse, Fagin's den and Mr Brownlow's home.

## POETRY

### Group activities

- Poetry presentations either performed live or on tape, including prepared readings and commentaries, to explore sounds and meaning. These can be thematically arranged, combining older and contemporary poems, or presented as a study of one poet.
- Wall displays of group anthologies with commentaries, poetry posters or storyboard/comic-strip versions of narrative poems such as 'The Rime of the Ancient Mariner', ballads, a 'Canterbury Tale'.

### Individual activities

- Individual anthology, either thematic or of one author, with commentaries and illustration.
- Poems 'modelled' on those read, e.g. ballads, odes, 'Prologue'-style portraits.
- Reports written of a group's discussions of a small selection of poems.
- Written comparisons of two poems on a similar theme: 'A narrow fellow in the grass' by Emily Dickinson and Lawrence's 'Snake'.

When pre-twentieth-century books have been read as core texts and individuals have read linked contemporary texts for themselves, there is scope for ambitious work to explore those links. Individual or pair projects could compare different treatments of the same theme, e.g. the relationship between races in *Huckleberry Finn, The Cay, Roll of Thunder Hear My Cry*; school life in *Tom Brown's Schooldays, Martini on the Rocks, Grange Hill* stories, etc.

No specific reference to pre-twentieth-century literature as part of GCSE has been made in this chapter. Teachers should feel more confident about introducing more difficult texts appearing as 'set books' when methods for working with them have been established with younger pupils. Equally, teachers who have planned for continuity and balance in their approach throughout the secondary phase find that pupils are equipped for the challenge of such texts and can respond with the confidence and immediacy of this 16-year-old writing of a crucial episode in *Great Expectations*.

> But at the end, when they part, despite being a fish out of water, Joe finds it in him to be kind to Pip. This is one of the most touching bits in the book. It shows that you can be without airs and graces, and money and manners, and flowered dressing gowns, and servants, and still be honest, and kind and care for someone. This, for me, is the whole skeleton of the book, and that is why the scene is important.

(Jackson, 1983)

## REFERENCES AND FURTHER READING

Jackson, D (1983) *Encounters With Books*, Methuen, London
Ogborn, J and Simons, M (1993) 'An interview with Graham Frater', *English and Media Magazine*, No. 28, Summer 1993, p. 8

Benton, M and Fox, G (1985) *Teaching Literature 9–14*, Oxford University Press, Oxford
Jeffcoate, R (1992) 'Dickens in the junior school', *English in Education*, Spring 1992, Vol. 26, No. 1
Merrick, B (1991) *Exploring Poetry 8–13*, National Association for the Teaching of English
Protherough, R (1983), *Developing Response to Fiction*, Open University Press, Milton Keynes
Shaw, C (1990) 'A language for exploring texts', *English in Education*, Autumn 1990, Vol. 24, No. 3
Stibbs, A (1993) 'The teacherly practice of literary theory', *English in Education*, Summer 1993, Vol. 27, No. 2

Chapter 5

# What is the range of writing?
Jan Sargeant

Writing forms only one aspect of the English curriculum but it is a crucially important one nonetheless. Prospective employers, examiners and the general public see the art of writing as the most fundamental test of a person's ability to communicate clearly and accurately. In speaking, the intonation, gesture, manner all add to the words spoken. If the audience does not understand, we can try again. We can enlarge and develop ideas, we can respond to questions from our audience. Within that relationship which exists between speaker and listener, we can strive until our meaning is clear. In writing, however, the author relies solely on the words themselves and 'any lapse from reasonable standards of legibility, spelling, vocabulary, syntax and punctuation creates a barrier between writer and reader' (Schools Council, 1983).

Though there is a direct link between speaking and writing, in that all writing systems first originated as a means of rendering speech into a fixed and visible format, writing is not merely the transcription of speech. Both have their own specialisms. In writing, there will be none of the interjections, stumbles, pauses or gesticulation which will arise in a conversation. The writer attempts to convey the information in such a way as to anticipate any searches for clarity on the part of the reader. This is why, in the early stages of drafting, it is often useful for children and teachers to act as responders to others' texts, so that they can ask the questions, such as 'How?', 'Why?' and 'Can you describe . . .?', which aid the writers to make their meaning or picture clearer and more effective. Some primary schools have adopted the practice of having double-page spreads for each piece of writing, whereby the writer writes on one side and a response partner, having read the piece, can write alongside questions requesting clarity or more information. In helping children understand the differences between speaking and writing, schemes of work can be undertaken which help make these more explicit; I shall return to this point later when looking at more practical suggestions.

## BECOMING WRITERS

My parents still have the first story I ever wrote at home when I was around 6 years old. For the purposes of illustrating early, formative writing, I include it here:

A girl went to the park. There was a wolf. It hid.
The wolf jumped out. It ate the girl. The end.

It was very simple in structure though it did have a clear beginning, middle and end. The presentation was poor, I was helped with the spellings and I am fairly confident that I could develop this story more fully nowadays, especially in consultation with a response partner. It does, though, show some evidence of basic syntax. Children acquire their syntax by a gradual process of refinement. In writing, as in speaking, short statements are gradually replaced by more sophisticated constructions. As teachers, we would expect a later version of this story to be far more developed in terms of sentence structure.

This also raises another consideration when developing children as writers. We would not only expect this story, with the same basic plot, to be written by an older child using more sophisticated syntax. We would also expect to see more detail in terms of description and perhaps dialogue; in fact, a more thorough understanding of the genre of short story writing.

There can also be seen in this story some indication of my early reading. Since there were no wolves in deepest Lancashire, I can only assume that the tale was informed by the fairy tales which formed part of my staple reading diet from being very young. This leads us to the other link which can be made with writing, that of reading.

Writing is nurtured by the experience of other texts. In reading, children have to sort the evidence of a spelling system, the conventions of punctuation and those conventions whereby we distinguish a fairy tale from a shop notice. Children will hear rhythm and rhyme when they read poetry. Becoming aware of such techniques and conventions will then inform their own writing. Much learning about writing is achieved through seeing the writing of others. This is not to suggest that children need to be able to read before they can write. Much formative work on letters can be done prior to reading as a development of drawing which itself is a development of play. Children are still drawn into reading their own work and receiving a response to it from adults and other children and thereby making the crucial connection between the two.

These connections between speaking, reading and writing are paramount in developing children as writers. They should all form an integral and integrated part of any classroom work on writing development. This idea of their integrated nature (given welcome emphasis in the 1995 programmes of study) can be hindered by artificial groupings into

Attainment Targets and, more recently, by the demise of Dual Award at Key Stage 4. It is the responsibility and challenge of teachers to help children make these connections and to use their abilities as speakers and readers to aid them in their own authorship.

Writing is not, of course, only confined to the English curriculum and one must always be conscious of its cross-curricular implications. This is somewhat easier to achieve and plan for in the primary schools where subject timetabling is far less stringent and the possibilities for thematic approaches exist, at present anyway. A great deal of exciting language work does happen in other subjects but this is more difficult to plan for in a secondary school. The idea of all teachers being teachers of language, if not English, is not one which has been met with much enthusiasm, especially in today's climate of unrest and stress. Given the reluctance of many teachers to take this on board, it is reassuring that children themselves are adept at transferring the skills of what happens in one subject to another. English teachers, whilst they must guard against being the 'service subject' for all others in terms of writing development, can play a vital role in enabling children to make such transfers and connections. It is important to remember that all children will be asked to produce many pages of writing throughout their school lives and probably less than a quarter will be in English lessons. Their quest for meaning and clarity, however, remains the same, regardless of the subject matter.

## REQUIREMENTS OF THE NATIONAL CURRICULUM

Turning back to the question of how we can develop children as confident, able writers and extend the range of their writing, there is a need to examine the English curriculum itself since it is through the delivery of the curriculum that we either help, or hinder, the child. When the first version of the National Curriculum Orders became standard legislation a few years ago, there was some early trepidation amongst English teachers. There was concern that such a statutory approach might stifle the creative work going on in schools (and by 'creative', I do not mean 'creative writing' in its popular sense); that, furthermore, it might be prescriptive in its demands of how to teach. Such concerns were largely allayed by the original (1989) version of the National Curriculum. Despite its limitations and the inherent problems of assessment, largely unresolved even now, it was received by many teachers as a positive affirmation of much valuable work actually happening in many schools and as a framework within which everyone could share and draw on good practice. As with any legislation, it remained for the people within the system to make it work for themselves and those in their care. It gave for the first time a national and clear indication of what elements were needed in an English curriculum, and was systematic in detailing the various activities and modes of learning. Looking back through much of the literature available prior to the Order, it does appear that there was a need for such information. In a Schools Council Working Paper (1983), attention was drawn to one school which had formulated a twenty-eight question checklist as to what constituted a good primary language programme. It states 'Despite its length the list does show most helpfully how varied and complex objectives are in this area of the curriculum' (p. 63). Yet, the questions relating to Writing are few:

Point 15:   Do children have enough time for continuous writing?
Point 16:   Are they encouraged to use various modes of expression for communicating ideas, information, stories and impressions?
Point 24:   Are children encouraged to produce handwriting which has aesthetic and decorative value? (p. 63)

The authors of this book suggest, 'There is evidence that many schools might improve the relevance, range and quality of their work by examining questions like these' (p. 64). This kind of advice, however intrinsically sound, did not offer teachers very much information about the wide variety of modes of writing which should be experienced by children. Whilst it did stress the integrated nature of language development, there was very limited input regarding Writing itself, apart from one other question which related to spelling and syntax.

Cox's report and the subsequent Orders for English remedied this. The Programmes of Study for both Key Stages 1 and 2 offered valuable ideas about the actual range of writing to be experienced. This range can be seen to develop throughout the remaining key stages, with obviously increasing emphasis on more sophisticated and even more varied form of language use. Both that version of the National Curriculum and those of the 1994 Proposals and 1995 place much stress on the wide variety of genres to be experienced by children in their reading and writing. Poetry, drama, narrative, chronological and non-chronological modes are all demanded by the Statutory Orders. Within the Programmes of Study, there is made evident the need to build on prior knowledge of these genres to develop a more sophisticated understanding of how each has its own appropriate register and conventions. Children are encouraged to read models of such genres and in their own writing to replicate these. Suggestions of 'range' at different Key Stages, however, appear to propose a different developmental approach. These seem to suggest that in fact some kind of sequential hierarchy of genres exists, whereby some modes are easier than others and should therefore be introduced at different stages, or levels.

Where schools are, rightly, ignoring such a suggestion and making efforts to introduce students to a wide range of genres, from an early age, problems arise when levels of attainment are decided upon at the end of the key stages. According to the junior schools with whom we work, children were coming to us with level 7 in AT3. Since level 7 corresponds to a good pass at GCSE, we, in the secondary phase, were highly doubtful of such achievements. It has taken many meetings where we share examples of work and cross-moderate to iron out such apparent discrepancies. Any genre, whether poetry, drama, narrative or discursive, ranges from simple to complex functions and involves abilities at different levels. This is why, in English, we can be said to be constantly 'revisiting' areas of the curriculum.

One of the most acute limitations of the 1989 Orders lay in the assessment of levels of attainment; the artificially produced grade levels were most limiting given that language acquisition does not follow such a logical and sequential pattern as the levels imply. (See chapter 6 on assessment for a more detailed examination of the issue.)

In his introduction to a report on the original Orders (Barrett *et al.*, 1992) John Johnson describes a joint survey by NATE and the National Association for Advisers in English which investigated the implementation of the National Curriculum in English throughout sixteen LEAs. It made a number of points worth bearing in mind. About AT3, it says:

- increasing demands and challenges were being made of children as writers
- a greater range of tasks was set
- basic writing skills were receiving satisfactory attention
- writing skills seemed best developed in the context of the child's own writing

With regard to AT4/5:

- many schools had moved towards improved policies on the teaching of spelling and handwriting
- handwriting and presentation were being given satisfactory attention.

However, this survey also confirmed HMI findings that standards of writing, whilst satisfactory, were less high than in the other ATs, especially at KS2, where 'In particular, the drafting of written work was often superficial, being too readily confined to making fair copies, without including shaping.' Such criticisms of the way in which some schools are implementing the Orders need to be addressed.

Any revisions to the Orders should refer back to the National Writing Project. This project emphasises the range of different skills and experiences which form 'basic writing skills'. It affirmed that whilst grammatical knowledge is needed, this can be acquired and developed in a wide variety of ways, as can spelling competence. The valuable work produced by the LINC project itself is indicative of the many strategies teachers can employ to avoid decontextualised exercises on aspects of technical skills.

The work of the LINC project and the National Writing Project suggests firmly that such learning must take place within a coherent, integrated scheme of work. Decontextualised exercises bear little resemblance to real writing, nor are they proven ways of developing knowledge about language. Cox, writing in the NATE publication (Barrett *et al.*, 1992), speaks of the valuable work which has been undertaken on grammar and knowledge about language and calls the government's stopping of this research 'a disgrace' (p. 16). There is no doubt that many teachers have found the ideas in the publications arising from this research to be both refreshing and effective in developing children's understanding of how language works and allowing them control over its varied rhetorical conventions.

The 1994 Proposals – now fortunately amended – seemed to suggest that until children have mastered the basic writing skills, they cannot produce writing which conveys meaning. Such a reductionist stance is at odds with what we know of the process of writing development. The increased emphasis on skills is one of the most contentious issues surrounding the proposals. Michael Armstrong (*Times Educational Supplement*, 18 May 1993) talks about 'The careful distinction which the current Order makes between compositional and secretarial skills'. In the new proposals a much greater emphasis is laid on the product of writing as opposed to the process. There is a cursory mention of drafting and little mention of the use of IT. Drafting is noted in the POS from KS2 but within that for KS3 there is also the proviso that 'Pupils should be taught to write with fluency and, on occasions, speed'. Pupils should also 'learn to judge the extent to which they need to use any or all of these processes in specific pieces of work' – this is in relation to the statements regarding the process of drafting at KS3. When one considers the increased emphasis on terminal examinations and the demise of coursework in KS4, there will be a real temptation for teachers to place increasing emphasis on 'speed writing' and to move away from the 'revising process' which 'real' writers use.

There is a clear emphasis throughout the proposed level descriptions and POS on the secretarial skills of writing. Certainly, such proposals would make it more difficult for children to succeed in the Writing attainment target given that it would encompass all these skills as well as compositional ones. Children with special educational needs are not exactly being offered an 'entitlement' curriculum here.

It would be too easy to fall victim to the feelings of powerlessness as an English teacher caught up in this debate but if we can hold strongly our beliefs about what is at the heart of good English teaching, the paths through whatever form a national curriculum eventually takes will be clearer.

## THE RANGE OF WRITING IN SCHOOLS

So far, I have examined some of the more fundamental points to bear in mind when developing a writing programme in schools. The concept of integrated activities, incorporating speaking and listening, reading, writing and knowledge about language skills, is paramount for the reasons outlined. Another primary concern also underpins the teaching of Writing. When looking closely at all the literature available, including the existing and proposed Orders, three words tie together the compositional and secretarial aspects of writing – form, audience and purpose. In days when it is fashionable to coin a new acronym for anything educational, they can collectively be known as the FAP factor. Whenever a new piece of writing is set for children in my classes, I write FAP on the board in large letters as a reminder of the parameters they must decide upon before putting pen to paper. In fact, we are all implicitly aware of FAP when crafting any piece of writing and that awareness informs our decisions, so that we know, for example, that whilst we draft a letter of application or to the bank manager, we need not do the same for a note requesting more milk.

Writers always write within a situation. That situation frames their response. Offering children, via their reading and own writing, a wide variety of modes gives them a repertoire on which to draw in their later authorship. These modes should cover transactional, expressive and poetic, although they do necessarily at times overlap. For example, an 'argument' may well be in the form of a playscript, a poem or a letter. One of my own colleagues, Valerie Murrey, produced an excellent scheme of work on 'Argument' as part of a research project at Hull University. She took Gender Stereotyping as a theme with a Year 7 class and drawing on a wide variety of stimuli, the children produced poems, posters and eventually letters to a toy manufacturer arguing against the stereotyped images to be found in their catalogue. (For a more detailed account, see Murrey, 1992.)

It is important to note that in setting this writing task, Valerie asked the students to write to a real toy manufacturer and actually sent their letters, since it was in the creation of a real context and audience that she enabled them to write letters which were 'all of a high quality' (Andrews *et al.*, 1993). Children's awareness of audience is an important factor in their development as writers. To create a real audience such as this, however, is not always possible, but there are ways in which teachers can extend the audiences for their students' writing, other children hearing the work produced, for example. In some schools, a large ring-binder is kept in the classroom, with plastic wallets into which children can slot recent pieces for others to see. The use of display boards, regularly changed and preferably with some outside the classroom, is another way in which children's writing can be brought to the notice of others, and a very real way in which the importance of final presentation and legibility can be made clear.

Sometimes the creation of an audience beyond the usual student/ teacher relationship is made possible by writing in role. For my own part in the 'Argument' project, I wrote to the students in the role of Chief Wizard, one of the characters in the novel we used as a springboard, *Equal Rites* by Terry Pratchett. They then had to write back to 'me' arguing against 'my' decision. The pieces of writing produced on this occasion were all highly fluent and well structured, drawing on all the information gained over the previous weeks. (See Andrews *et al.*, 1993, p. 135; Sargeant, 1993.)

The awareness of the audience does not simply create contexts for children's writing. It also informs their decisions, regarding purpose: is the writing to entertain, describe, instruct, for example? This in turn leads back to the form. So although there are three elements of the FAP factor, they are in fact very closely interrelated. They inform part of our own criteria for assessment and they are crucial aspects of successful writing.

## DEVELOPING A PRACTICAL WRITING PROGRAMME

What I wish to do now is to illustrate one further way in which these fundamental tenets behind the teaching of writing can be applied practically in the English classroom. This is not because I feel it to be an exemplary approach but because the project outlined ties together many of the principles with which I have dealt so far and clearly reflects the way in which a path can be negotiated through the legislation and guidance pressing around us.

In September 1990, I began work with my Year 10 students on their GCSE coursework, which itself was prescribed within certain boundaries by its examination nature. I wanted to give these students the experience of writing for a real audience, in a variety of ways, and furthermore to permit them ownership of their writing and control over the writing process. Being new to the school and to the locality, I was curious about my new home. Also Withernsea is a small coastal town whose population doubles during August with the many tourists who go there, known as 'diggers' locally. There seemed to be much opportunity for a book about how Withernsea used to be, not just for the locals but for people like me, new to the area, as well as the tourists. BP Exploration at Easington were prepared to fund the publication of such a book and the students were given their brief. They had, through interviews with the local community, to produce a book covering a range of writing about how Withernsea used to be years ago. I arranged for Wendy Blair, then editor of the local newspaper, the *Gazette*, to come into school to help give a course on interviewing, including listening skills and recording techniques. The students then advertised through the *Gazette* for willing interviewees.

Two of these people turned out to have moved to Dorset, so the two students responsible for these interviews had to rearrange very quickly their proposed format and decisions were made to use letters, questionnaire and audio tapes through the post. The class had already divided into pairs and small groups, feeling the need for back-up as support in their interviewing of strangers and very much aware of the transcription time which would be necessary. Whilst the interviews were being completed out of school hours, we spent time in class looking at a variety of textual sources: poetry, stories, media formats for recording interviews with pop singers and the like. We explored the ways in which these differed, their respective potential and limitations. By reading others' texts, a repertoire of possible forms was developed. Analyses and deconstruction of these models for writing would ultimately serve to allow students to reconstruct their own versions of such texts.

The transcriptions of the recorded interviews took a good few lessons, with small groups dotted about the school in classrooms for privacy. They found the task onerous but essential. I mentioned earlier the ways whereby the differences between speech and writing can be made more explicit to children and this kind of transcription is one of these methods. In having to write down every pause, every stumble and the exact wording for selected pieces from their interviews, the students very quickly realised that to process the interviews into a written format, there was much work to do. This kind of active involvement in and 'playing around with' language is when much learning takes place. They had decided earlier that for the purposes of a book rather than a magazine, the question and answer format was unsuitable so they had to devise means by which their information could be imparted without the questions which prompted it. They also realised that they would have to omit some words, add others and sometimes change word order for their written versions to conform to the requirements for written English. In this way, understanding of syntax was developed. Since we do not very often speak in sentences, the need for punctuation and demarcation into complete sentences was explored far more vigorously than usual by the students themselves.

A further 'problem' arose when they came to look at the actual language. They wanted to retain the flavour of individual voices, believing this to be an important element in any book on any locality, but they were increasingly aware that people such as myself had needed to have translations of certain terminology, such as 'diggers' when I had first heard the tapes. So the question of dialect versus Standard English arose quite naturally out of this quest for clarity for their audience.

We took two lessons out at this stage to examine the differences between the two forms of language and the potential limitations of dialect in the written and spoken forms. I enlisted the help in this of Jenny Cobley, an Advisory Teacher for English in Humberside and closely involved in the LINC project. The idea of 'Teachers as resources' was becoming built-in to the project by this time. The students were forming the questions based upon their own experimentation with language, they were deciding upon the help they required. As an active participant and observer, I was also aware when intervention and assistance were needed, but they retained the ownership over their work, and it was this control, I believe, which culminated in the final, polished work and their ongoing commitment to it. Having devised initially the parameters and the context within which they would work, my role had ceased to be that of instigator and controller, and had developed instead into that of an enabler.

They decided that for their intended audience, the book would need to be written in Standard English – in other words, they accepted that Standard English 'has come to have a wide social and geographical currency and to be the form most frequently used . . . in writing' (detailed provision for KS2). They found ways around retaining some of the local dialect and flavour – they could write notes at the end of pieces with dialect translations. They could, they felt, still use dialect in their poems, since the poetic form offered more scope for different language use yet was still seen as 'valid' in the eyes of the public, as proven by their reading of Creole and West Indian poetry.

Working in pairs and small groups also aided them in their drafting. Not only could they allocate different tasks or parts to each other but they could then act as response partners for each other's work. Their shared knowledge about language, its conventions, spelling system and syntax was invaluable at this stage.

Some of the more able students were used as final proof-readers by those less sure of their spelling or punctuation and a great deal of mutual support, teaching and learning went on at this point. Their awareness all the time that this was to be potentially for an outside audience made them very much readier to be constructively critical of what they read. I played my part in this also, of course, and regular feedback was provided in this way for every student. Having said this, there were still errors which had to be corrected at the final editing stage by myself, but this could not be done until they had submitted their work initially as part of their GCSE coursework. The mutual collaboration which did occur I cannot see as 'cheating' in the way that critics of coursework examinations suggest – children are still tested in examination conditions as part of their coursework assessment and collaboration amongst members of any society is generally seen to be most fruitful. Having submitted their final copies for their coursework, copies were then submitted to the 'editorial panel' they had elected. I was allowed a role in this though I cannot even now decide whether this was because I had proved myself to be invaluable or whether it was because, underneath their sense of ownership, the teacher/pupil dynamics still operated, as they do in every classroom. I would like to think it was the former; I believe it may have been the latter.

When the final decisions had been made, they elected a new group who would be responsible for the subsequent presentation and transfer onto disk. Again, outside help was enlisted, this time from BP Exploration who brought not only expertise but also a more sophisticated DTP (Desk Top Publishing) program. The book was published almost a year after we had started work. At its official launch, much was made by those present of the 'product' of the project. It was indeed, and remains, an impressive testament of what can be achieved by a group of young writers. For myself, however, it was my own awareness of how much had gone into the process of its creation which made an even greater impact. This process can be summarised in the following way:

CONTEXT CREATED
⇓
CONTROL GIVEN TO STUDENTS
⇓                      ⇓

SPEAKING AND LISTENING        READING OF OTHERS' TEXTS
(INTERVIEWS)                      (MODELS FOR WRITING)
⇓                            ⇓

ANALYSES OF DIFFERENCES IN     WIDE REPERTOIRE OF FORMS
SPEECH AND WRITING
⇓

STANDARD ENGLISH DIALECT
⇓

DRAFTING
⇓

REVISION                     COLLABORATION, SUPPORT AND
⇓                       CRITICISM FROM PEERS AND
LOOKING AT LANGUAGE SKILLS           TEACHER
NEEDED

⇓
FINAL PRODUCT
⇓                       ⇓

WIDER AUDIENCE NEEDS CLEARER     ASSESSMENT BY TEACHER
PRESENTATION
⇓

BOOK FORM IS REALISED
⇓

ON SALE IN SHOPS

## SUMMARY

I have made much of the need for children to have control over what they write and to retain their sense of ownership. As teachers, we must allow for this to happen, but remember also that this does not mean that children themselves should be the ones to decide exactly what they write and when. We all only write within contexts. If we left children with their more limited knowledge of the varieties of contexts for writing, we would do them a disservice. It is the challenge of the English curriculum, and the teachers who deliver it, to create new and varied contexts for children's writing. The more meaningful these contexts are, the greater the scope for developing children as writers.

The teacher's role in this also necessarily involves that of assessment, but must extend beyond that potential limitation. Our primary response is as readers of children's texts, and should therefore be to what is being said. I thoroughly enjoy reading children's writings. My detailed comments at the end of their work substitute, too often regrettably, for personal, spoken dialogue, but some form of dialogue between writer and reader / child and teacher should form the basis for our assessment, or 'marking'. The levels or grades can come later. The correction of errors, similarly, should be sensitive. It should begin by looking for patterns behind errors and from this can come selective intervention and instruction on the areas causing the most problem. Within any class there will be widely varying levels of competence and confidence, and the extent of the correction should be directly proportionate to those levels.

One further point is that teachers, in order to remember the complexities of the writing process, should also write themselves. They ought to write for children to read, and they may also write for other outside audiences, as I do here. I remember as a naive and relatively inexperienced teacher, I once went to an INSET session on children's writing. A lecturer, from Birmingham University, walked into the room, and told us to write a story on space travel. Then she made us read it out, with no time to revise or draft. To this day, I can well feel my horror and shame. I would hope that in the intervening years, I have learned sufficiently never to make a child feel as I did then. 'If children see us writing, they are more likely to conclude that writing is worth the time and effort' (*The English Curriculum: Writing*, ILEA). Another of my colleagues reads a book whenever her class are having a private reading lesson for the same reason. I share the fact that I write with my students. I do not expect them to read everything but when I talk to them about the importance of drafting and shaping a piece, they know at least that I speak from personal experience.

Children want to communicate. Why else would they want to learn to talk? They also want to communicate on paper. Otherwise, they would not suffer the same frustrations that they do when their oral ability outshines their writing ability. They want to share their thoughts and opinions, their make-believe, with us. As a teacher of English, I still feel a sense of wonder at the skill and creativity children bring to their writing. I also feel a sense of honour and privilege that they share their creations with me. When we talk about extending the range of children's writing, we must remember that it is as the readers of their texts, not so much as their teachers, that we best enable them.

## REFERENCES AND FURTHER READING

Andrews, R, Costello, P and Clarke, S (1993) *Improving the Quality of Argument, 5–16*, University of Hull

Armstrong, M in *Times Educational Supplement*, 18 May 1993

Barrett, P, Cox, B and Dickinson, T (1992) *Made Tongue-tied by Authority: New Orders for English?*, NATE, Longman, Harlow

Brown, R and Belugi, U (1964) 'Three processes in the child's requisition of syntax', *Harvard Educational Review*, Vol. 34, No. 2

Burgess (1973) *Understanding Children Writing*, Penguin, Harmondsworth

ILEA (nd) *The English Curriculum: Writing*

Murrey, V (1992) 'Developing argument', *Theme* 5, Autumn 1992, pp. 21–4

Sargeant, J (1993) 'Gender and power: the meta-ethics of teaching argument in schools', *Curriculum*, Vol. 14, No. 1, 1993, pp. 6–13

Schools Council Working Paper 75, *Primary Practice* (1983) Methuen Educational, London

SCAA (1994) *English in the National Curriculum: Draft Proposal (May 1994)*, Schools Curriculum and Assessment Authority

# Chapter 6

# Can we assess and keep sane?

## A personal view

*Peter Brown*

---

## INTRODUCTION

The growing crisis which led up to the 1993 whole-scale boycott of government plans for the testing of 14-year-olds spawned a debate about the subject of assessment that was widespread, intense and often compelling. The continuing debate and changes to government plans during 1994 is clear evidence of how controversial an issue the assessment of the National Curriculum has become. That it should be English which led the opposition to the first year of extensive testing of 14-year-olds is not perhaps surprising. There may be some explanation for this in the nature of the subject itself; it is possible to speculate that it may even have something to do with the nature of the people who teach English and this is why a fairly clear consensus emerged among English teachers over their response to the government's assessment proposals. Ministers made a serious misjudgement in the period leading up to the first boycott through being unable to foresee that the vast majority of teachers of English would hold faith to a rationale for English teaching which had evolved out of years of continuous professional debate and which, when the subject was in crisis, enable teachers to speak with a remarkably unified voice.

As the testing issue first began to acquire a political focus, changing faces at the Department for Education and within the key advisory bodies meant that, in a few short months, CAT-style SATs were out, teacher assessment had been slashed from proposed KS4/GCSE syllabuses to be replaced by 'pencil and paper tests' along with prescribed texts and tiered levels of entry. This was always a particularly vindictive and calculated bit of legislation in that it deliberately imposed constraints upon the ability of schools to arrange their pupils in the grouping systems that they deemed appropriate. The fact that the categories of entry were different (and more restrictive) in English from those in the other subjects made clear that the attack was particularly aimed at the tradition of teacher assessment which had been probably more prominent in English than any other subject.

Those who opposed these constraints argued that the testing arrangements had important implications for the curriculum that was being taught in the months leading up to Year 9 tests. Many schools for example had great experience in the teaching of Shakespeare across a wide band of ability and wished to continue to do so but were prevented from so doing by the test regulations. The arrogance of those who were essentially outside the profession deciding that certain areas of literature could be taught to one particular range of pupils whilst ignoring the experience of the professionals was once again clearly on display. The revision of these restrictions for the 1994 tests was at least a positive development and perhaps the first sign that after all even the politicians (particularly while Sir Ron Dearing was holding their hands) could learn to listen to what others were saying.

Even before the final capitulation in the summer of 1993, with Sir Ron Dearing brought in to do the job that the Secretary of State for Education should have been doing, the fact that senior subject advisers were abandoning ship and some key government appointees were distancing themselves from beleaguered ministers and denouncing the very system that they had been instrumental in setting up in the first place, must have seriously undermined the confidence of ministers. This confidence must have been further weakened by the unanimity of the dissent coming from both the independent and state sectors in their opposition to the tests, and particularly the English tests. As early as December 1992 came reports in the *Times Educational Supplement* of a swingeing attack on aspects of government policy from such surprising quarters as the Conservative chairman of the Commons Select Committee on Education who spoke of the danger of the 'bigots' and 'extremists' of the influential pressure groups who seemed to have regular access to the ministerial ear. He characterised them as being 'lords of misrule' spreading 'insidious propaganda'. The *Mail On Sunday* for 31 January 1993 (with ministerial fingerprints seemingly all over it) carried a ludicrous report on the activities of the National Association for the Teaching of English declaring: 'Marxist teachers aiming to wreck education plans'. The desperation of the government was plain for all to see.

Meanwhile the terminology had changed too: Standard Assessment 'Tasks' had become Standard Assessment 'Tests' and 'assessment' had become 'testing'. Crucially, debate had stopped. Any pretence that there was any dialogue was gone. Education policy was administered with a firm grip from the top.

A major consequence of this was to produce a new solidarity of dissatisfied teachers from a range of subject areas and key stages. Head teacher organisations, parent groups and some notably enlightened governing bodies may take justifiable credit for widening and managing the discontent felt by teachers. Together they faced ministers whose apparent arrogance and failure to listen had seemed to them to have alienated even the most moderate of teachers so comprehensively that, by the time the teaching unions and professional organisations eventually took up the issue on a national scale and confronted the legal ramifications of the boycott, they overwhelmingly rejected the government's plans for assessment and testing at 14. The rest, as they say, is history.

But that history includes the beginnings of a change in government's approach when we take into account the successful national boycott of testing in 1993 and the decision by government to bring in an outside trouble shooter. The Department for Education was in retreat and the Secretary of State was in bed. The arrival of Sir Ron Dearing's interim report on *The National Curriculum and its Assessment* did at last introduce a new climate of rational dialogue. The final Dearing Report which was accepted by the Secretary of State, and the publication of the 1995 English curriculum, suggested that some of the aspirations of the profession might yet be fulfilled. Clearly whatever has been achieved cannot be seen other than in the context of the boycott and the momentum generated by the campaign against the SATs. In essence we are talking about the collective wish of English teachers to retain the integrity of their subject and the effects of a successful campaign to make it clear that a whole regime of misguided tests was resting on a discredited, dangerous dogma. Without that boycott and the lead provided by English teachers, there would have been no Dearing review, no voice of reason and little prospect of peace or stability in schools for the foreseeable future.

For teachers of English most of the arguments against the SATs in 1994 were as pertinent as they had been in 1993, yet it was harder to defend the continuation of the boycott into a second year, particularly since the solidarity of the professional associations had already dissolved, and there was a more conciliatory atmosphere of concessions and consultation engendered by Sir Ron Dearing's influence. Nevertheless, there was a growing sense of vindication for the scepticism of English teachers in their initial reaction to the new curriculum arising from the SCAA proposals. Indeed, perhaps nothing much has changed: true, they proposed still to have two tests albeit this was half of the original number, and there was a more rational approach to differentiated papers. Even as teachers began to talk ominously about 'accountability', even 'legislation', most English departments would have felt confident that the English Orders were broadly in line with the type of curriculum they wished to deliver and, with certain adjustments, were as likely as not already teaching towards.

By the time the Draft Proposal was issued in May 1994 it was still clear that notwithstanding Sir Ron's listening ear, teachers' voices were not yet

heard as distinctly as the voices of politicans. Teachers have been consulted but overruled it seems on many a contentious point. Sir Ron sought
to elevate the professional judgement of teachers yet still felt the need to
issue a reading list to English teachers just in case there should be any
doubt about how that professional judgement should be exercised.

## ASSESSMENT AFTER DEARING

In Sections 1.11–1.21. of his interim report, *The National Tests and Teacher
Assessment*, Sir Ron Dearing rightly states that teacher assessment lies,

> at the heart of the learning process in that new learning must be
> matched to what a pupil already knows and can do. It is the teacher in
> his/her classroom who, day in day out, undertakes this vitally import-
> ant task of formative assessment.

Nothing much wrong with that. Yet, whilst he goes on to concede that,
'Properly moderated teacher assessment can also contribute important
summative information about a pupil's achievements', it is undoubtedly,
for Sir Ron, the national tests which will 'provide a reliable means of
establishing levels of achievement by pupils in schools throughout the
country'. He asserts this because the tests are 'standard'. However, just
how reliable they will prove to be as indicators of performance depends
on whether or not they are good tests in the first place and whether or not
they reflect the type of learning and assessment processes that operate in
the classroom. There is also the danger that the tests will focus on what is
easiest to test, not what is most appropriate to test. If this is the case then
the testing arrangements will exert a considerable influence upon what is
taught.

Whilst Sir Ron Dearing's Curriculum Review and SCAA's subsequent
Draft Proposals for English may have satisfied the demands of many
teachers for an upgrading of the role of teacher assessment, Sir Ron
retains an unshakeable belief in the efficacy of 'national tests'. Furthermore it seems that the price that teachers must pay for the raising of the
status of their assessments is an acceptance of the accountability that
national tests will bring. There is still therefore the implication that it is
the national tests that are the 'rigorous' tests: moderated teacher assessment, according to Sir Ron, is something quite different. Just what does all
this mean? The 1993 tests were decidedly lacking in rigour. The Secretary of
State called for a sharper focus to be given to the tests. Were not those
who designed the tests attempting to provide this sharp focus?

Sir Ron's assertion that national tests raise standards by raising expectations begs a considerable question. It is good teaching that raises
standards not good testing. If Sir Ron needs any proof of this he need only
look at pupils' coursework. One suspects that most of the work

undertaken by Year 9 pupils studying the prescribed Shakespeare texts in 1993 and 1994 would have more than adequately prepared them for any test that SEAC could have devised because the majority of pupils were motivated to study the play by the quality of the learning experiences and assessment opportunities given to them, not because they were to be tested at the end of the process.

It is curious that teacher assessment should be given 'equal standing' to national tests, yet apparently cannot offer significant information about pupil performance in a summative function. In Section 5 of his report Sir Ron dismisses teacher assessment stating (he can hardly be said to have argued the point) that one can only have confidence in the process if it is moderated. The fact that teachers of English have successfully operated a reliable and effective system of moderated teacher assessment for over 15 years seems to have been overlooked by Sir Ron.

Any reduction in testing of course leaves more time for teaching and the reduction in papers from four to two frees the curriculum to some extent from the strait-jacket which the tests formerly imposed. The quiet passing of the Anthology will not be mourned. The piles of (probably unopened) packages of Anthologies are not only a sad reflection of the government's bullish insistence on pushing ahead with the tests in the face of the growing clamour for their revision, but a sad waste too. The whole ill-thought-out exercise is also evidence of the arrogance of those who presumed to be able to select from the vast canon of literature that which was somehow ripe for testing. Consequently we had little snippets of Dickens, yanked from huge and great works and plonked entirely out of context on the pages of an examination booklet; and, amidst the fondly cherished favourites of a few dons, worthy of a far greater exploration than that made possible by the tests, were the tired, old, predictable chestnuts which had been hoiked from someone's dim and distant memories of the classroom.

And, it is as well to remember that without the teachers' boycott of the tests the Anthology would undoubtedly be with us still. It is also hard to resist the thought that the spirit of this narrow vision is alive and well and living in the reading lists of the latest curriculum.

In the real world of the classroom and the secondary school department teaching materials are sensitively linked to the needs of pupils and it is possible to teach a wide range of demanding texts if the tasks given are appropriate and properly differentiated. External and arbitrarily imposed anthologies designed to test pupils will rarely work. For a start they can neither genuinely reflect what the pupil has learned about the text nor begin to quantify what they have carried away with them as part of the experience of reading literature.

Newland English department has devised its own 'Anthology' for

Year 9 pupils based on a series of poems suggested by one of the department's members. It is, like the SATs Anthology, thematically devised – though this selection does have the advantage of at least being coherent. These often demanding poems by such poets as Louis MacNiece, DH Lawrence, Ted Hughes, William Wordsworth, Seamus Heaney and others are offered to pupils (taught in their mixed-ability groups moreover) for their consideration and responses. Pupils discuss the poems in various grouping arrangements, make notes, answer questions, and write in various ways in response to the poems. Some of this material has already been linked to an 'Autobiography' topic followed by Year 9 pupils. This is part of the way the work of a department grows and develops.

＼ Sir Ron Dearing has conceded that the ten-level scale, as defined by the original statements of attainment (and imposed as a universal model for all subjects), has failed to provide a rational and workable framework for quantifying achievement in English. The Cox Committee had itself acknowledged that tying skills to levels in such a restrictive way could not reflect the fact that language development was a recursive process and that language skills were not acquired in this neat, linear way but were constantly being experienced and refined in different learning contexts. The arbitrary and often inconsistent model of progression through the strands and levels became all too clear. However, teachers were expected to devise recording systems in the face of these deficiencies. Like many English departments we at Newland struggled with these issues. An early assessment record sheet is included here (see appendix A). Developed conscientiously and in good faith it actually exposes the flaws in the assessment model quite effectively. Numbers appear and disappear because statements simply do not exist to cover the strand at that level. Though based on faulty premises in the respect that it was entirely drawn from the flawed ten-level scale and derived from pure National Curriculum speak, it at least served the useful purpose of easily proving evidence of assessment.

Any examination of the changing versions of statements of attainment, from Cox onwards, will demonstrate how inconsistent they were and how misleading were the supposed hierarchies of skills. The proposal to replace statements of attainment with level descriptions is indeed significant. However, it is ironic that the CATS Development Group provided participating schools with 'Assessment Criteria' for Key Stage 3 testing as long ago as 1991. What's more, English teachers have worked with the Examination Board's level descriptions as an assessment tool for years. SCAA have also come rather late to the idea that 'it is the programmes of study which should guide the planning, teaching and day to day assessment of pupils' work'. However, it is surely more sensible and realistic to move away from the 'plethora of detailed statements of attainment' to a more rational and workable system of 'levelness'. The emphasis here is on balance and professional judgement where teachers are encouraged to assess their pupils in a more rounded way, recognising that strengths in one area will be mediated by deficiencies elsewhere. Indeed, the level descriptions themselves at times reflect the often imprecise nature of the assessment process. Pupils will 'usually', 'generally' or 'often' demonstrate the features of language being considered.

The new eight-level scales of 'characteristic' performance may work, although the suggestion of neat progression through the levels and between Key Stages is still dubious. While conceding the argument for keeping Key Stage 4 separate, the 1995 programmes have missed the opportunity of providing eight-level scales for each Key stage, so overcoming the problems involved in assessing pupils on the same scale without being able to take into account the age-related factors at work, the level of maturity of the pupils and the nature of the tasks being set at different Key stages.

## A RATIONALE FOR ASSESSMENT

That assessment continues to be so controversial an issue perhaps has something to do with the fact that there has never been a clear enough definition about the reasons why we assess and for whom we assess. Part of the problem surely lies in the fact that the tests are seen to be capable of doing so many things by so many interested parties.

One guiding principle is that assessment should reflect the curriculum being taught and not direct it. This balance seemed to have shifted under the assessment requirements of the National Curriculum. Not only were the texts now being chosen by an outside agency, but also, because the testing system was emphasising ways of working which were unfamiliar to pupils, as many observers pointed out, the tests were not rooted in the curriculum itself.

Perhaps it is not so much the lack of a clear definition that is the problem but the fact that assessment is a single term for a many-headed beast. Assessment may be used for diagnostic purposes, assessing the individuals' strengths and weaknesses, the level they have achieved and their future learning needs; assessment may also be called upon to be predictive in terms of selecting pupils and informing decisions about 'tiers of entry'; assessment may also be required to perform a comparative function, ranking individuals in relation to their own progress as well as in relation to others or notional norms; assessment is now also being seen as a way of evaluating teaching and learning and, of course, the performances of schools. No test will achieve all these purposes at once.

Indeed, it is difficult to see how these assessment modes could ever be compatible.

Classroom teachers are making judgements about pupils' work all the time. They are therefore not averse to assessing pupils' work. Teachers intervene in the work of their pupils in order to enable them to make progress. In English the emphasis in all written work should be the purposeful and enjoyable activity of improving the quality of both expression and ideas, a part of which will be a concern with technical accuracy. This is what drafting is and pupils and teachers should be repeatedly engaged in the process. Speaking and listening and reading activities are also central to it.

It is a fundamental part of the business of assessment because it is part of the working process of the classroom. It is also part of the process by which pupils are encouraged to aim for higher standards.

Assessment that is geared only to identifying success or failure in supposedly objective terms makes little impact on the future learning of the pupils tested and should therefore not come to exercise a disproportionate influence on classroom activities.

A great deal of the teacher's input in the classroom at Newland School is, as far as possible, to work individually with pupils on drafts of written work. At the end of a piece of work a summative judgement is made in that it is marked. A level is not offered as it does not seem particularly helpful or meaningful to pupils. Just how reassuring is the placing of 'level 6' on the perfectly adequate work of a Year 9 pupil if that pupil can only see the 'grade' in terms of a ten-level scale? Positive comments are made and, where appropriate, points for consideration in future work are noted. At the end of a series of pieces of work or a Unit of Work a more formal assessment is made on all the attainment objectives covered in the topic and recorded on a uniform record sheet. In the same way Reading assessments are made and so too are comments about the Speaking and Listening activities which have been undertaken, and assessments are made and recorded where appropriate.

Although these recording systems were put in place specifically for the purpose of KS3 assessment the system is equally applicable to KS4 and the same sheets are used for Year 10 and Year 11 pupils. We are also attempting to provide an assessment record for the speaking and listening activities undertaken in Year 7, 8 and 9 Drama lessons. It remains to be seen how useful this is in assessment terms. However, it is a way of giving pupils credit for appropriate and valid achievements in another subject area and as a supplementary record it should give further information to the English teacher who must make the summative assessment at the end of KS3. A similar system is proposed for the cross-referencing of English activities for IT assessment. The proposed change of focus from statements of attainment to level descriptions will make these record sheets (in their present format) redundant. Yet further revisions will be required.

In addition to the marking policy noted above, assessment has been linked to the department's Record of Achievement system. This involves pupils in recording the work they have done, assessing their performance and identifying future targets. Pupils complete record sheets at the end of each Unit of Work or half term period and, at the end of each term, complete a Termly Review in an effort to encourage them to make judgements about their progress in the subject. The whole system sits, though very uneasily in places it must be said, within the school's overall Assessment, Recording and Reporting Policy.

The assessment and recording scheme outlined above, in varying forms, will be replicated in hundreds of English departments up and down the country. The record-keeping systems which operate within the department at Newland have been subject to constant and ongoing review. This situation has been in part a response to a whole succession of changing goal posts, but mainly because, in practice, these records have often proved inadequate for the job they were designed to do.

The first efforts, often primitive and handwritten (and sadly photo-copied in their thousands), have been replaced by more sophisticated forms as the word processing skills of those drawing up the documents have developed. The early problems generally arose out of the hopelessly unreasonable consumption of teacher time the systems devoured as colleagues attempted to perform the relatively familiar task of marking but found that the amount of form filling and paper shuffling involved produced acute apoplexy in normally rational men and women. The most destructive element of this was that of duplication. One particularly irrational early version of our system, for example, required teacher comments to be noted on specially designed teacher record sheets. A further comment, often the same one, was placed on a pupil record sheet. Not surprisingly, this system was abandoned just before it collapsed.

Following Sir Ron Dearing's Interim Report, department thinking on its recording and assessment processes shifted somewhat and, in the spirit of his recommendations, a far more rational document was put in place. This pre-empted, as it turned out later, the principle in the Draft Proposals in that, instead of being tied in to all the statements of attainment, the revised record sheet would identify general areas within the attainment targets against which assessments could be made (see appendix B). The system was adopted for use with both KS3 and KS4 pupils and, incidentally, satisfied the school's OFSTED inspection of February 1994.

The final piece of the recording armoury of the Newland department is the English Planning Sheet. This has proved invaluable in performing a number of useful tasks. It is principally a record of all learning and assessment activities but it also acts as a way of monitoring and explaining the teacher's particular approach to addressing the department's shared objectives and thereby the National Curriculum itself. In these days of accountability it is also felt that it is a valuable record for both individual teachers and heads of department to have (see appendix C).

There is little doubt that if we really are to 'keep sane' it is essential that assessment and recording systems remain rational, manageable and sensible. There was a time in the debate about the National Curriculum and assessment when the greatest heresy that an English teacher could utter was that of a willingness to tick boxes. It was as if by so doing one would deny pupils their worth. Such an understandable concern did not really take into account the fact that the assessment model that teachers were presented with was itself fundamentally flawed. Many subjects have indeed gone down the road of finding evidence for and recording the multitude of statements of attainment contained in their Orders. One suspects that there may have been rather less of this happening in English departments because most teachers of the subject recognised that it was an absurd and ultimately fruitless exercise.

However, given that teachers are required to record achievement in numerical terms and given the inherent deficiencies in the model, surely it is only sensible and realistic that the recording system must satisfy this requirement as painlessly as possible to all concerned. At Newland we eventually ticked boxes with the best of them. It all had very little to do with maximising the learning opportunities of pupils. In this respect it is the curriculum that really matters; this is where the energy of teachers must be directed and where they must stand firm, particularly against methods of assessment that work against pupils by reducing the quality of that curriculum.

Sir Ron Dearing's wish for a less bureaucratic system of recording assessments, manifested in the change to level descriptions, was foreshadowed in his letter to headteachers (*The Times Educational Supplement* 10 September 1993) when he wrote that:

> Judgements of whether a pupil is working at a particular level do not depend on ticking off every statement of attainment associated with the level; they depend on the teacher's assessment of which level best corresponds to the pupil's performance as a whole, using the statements of attainment as a guide.

This removal of the requirement to record the full range of statements of attainment was indeed a highly significant statement. It was rather disingenuously claimed at the time that this situation had only ever arisen because of a fundamental misunderstanding on the part of the profession created by the misplaced zeal of teachers: a curious sort of 'mass assessment hysteria'. This is hardly credible. Elaborate systems of recording were put in place in many subjects (and in English to some extent) because it was assumed to be part of the professional duty of teachers to do just that. Senior Management Teams expected it because it was being indicated to them that OFSTED would wish to see such systems in place. Sir Ron's common sense view of things will bring some much needed perspective to the reporting and recording issue but it should not be forgotten just how much work has already been done and revising recording systems yet again is not a prospect that anyone will particularly relish.

As for the likelihood of remaining sane through these uncertain times, teachers of English may well appear to have exhibited many of the manifestations of madness as they succumbed in turn to irrational hatred, paranoia, deep depression and anxiety! They may now be beginning to benefit from a year of therapy and consultation; they may have experienced moments of hysterical, maniacal laughter and vivid, frightening visions of marauding skipfuls of ring-binders, but those teachers are still here and will not be going away.

As both major political parties now seem committed to the concept of national testing, professional concerns have to focus on the precise nature of the tests, the purposes to which they are being put, and the extent to which – as Sir Ron Dearing asserted – classroom assessments are given the same status. It hardly seems realistic to expect one set of tests to achieve the many diverse functions that are currently being attributed to them. As this book reached proof stage, the government announced details of a 'Dearing-style' review of curriculum testing, involving regional conferences, independent audits of the tests, and on-the-spot evaluations by the Office for Standards in Education (including the effects of using external markers). Time will tell whether this belated concern for consultation manages to produce consensus within the profession.

## REFERENCES AND FURTHER READING

Johnstone, Brian (1987) *Assessing English: Helping Students to Reflect on Their Work*, Open University Press, Milton Keynes
Leach, Jenny and MacGregor, Val (1992) 'Making the transition: towards a secondary language record', *The English and Media Magazine*, No. 26, pp. 27–30
McGregor, Robert and Meiers, Marian (1991) *Telling the Whole Story*, Australian Council for Educational Research, Hawthorn, Victoria
Neville, Mary (1988) *Assessing and Teaching Language*, Macmillan Education, London
Protherough, Robert (1993) 'More absurd than in other subjects? Assessing English Literature', *English in Education*, Vol. 27, No. 1, pp. 10–18

SCAA (1994) *English in the National Curriculum: Draft Proposals*, Schools Curriculum & Assessment Authority
Stibbs, Andrew (1979) *Assessing Children's Language*, Ward Lock, London
Thornton, Geoffrey (1986) *APU Language Testing 1979-1983*, DES
White, Edward M (1985) *Teaching and Assessing Writing*, Jossey-Bass, San Francisco

## APPENDIX A

### NEWLAND SCHOOL FOR GIRLS
### National Curriculum: English Key Stage 3 Attainment Targets

Name .................... Form ....... Teacher ............

Unit .................................. Date ..............

**EN1        SPEAKING AND LISTENING**

| | | | | | | | | |
|---|---|---|---|---|---|---|---|---|
| Share personal experiences | 3a | | 5a | | | | | |
| Convey a simple message | 3b | | | | | | | |
| Give an account | | | 5a | 6b | 7b | 8b | 9a | 10a |
| Give and receive explanations, information and ideas | 3d | 4a | 5c | 6b | 7b | 8b | | |
| Express/argue a point of view | | 4c | 5b | 6a | 7a | 8a | 9a | 10a |
| Group discussion | 3c | 4c | 5b | 6a | 7c | 8c | 9b | 10b |
| Ask/respond to questions | | 4b | | | | | | |
| Presentation/performance | | 4b | 5d | 6c | | | 9a | |
| Knowledge about language | | | 5e | 6d | 7d | 8d | 9c | 10c |

Comments



EN4  SPELLING              3    4

EN5  HANDWRITING           3    4

EN   PRESENTATION                    5    6    7

4/5

**EN2 READING**

| Read aloud | 3a | 4a | | | | | | |
|---|---|---|---|---|---|---|---|---|
| Sustained silent reading | 3b | | | | | | | |
| Read a range of materials | 3a | 4a | 5a | 6a | 7a | 8a | 9a | 10a |
| Make a natural response to what is read | | | 5b | | 7b | 8b | 9b | 10b |
| Talk about aspects of reading | 3c | 4b | 5a | 6a | | | | |
| Respond to non-literary texts | | | 5c | 6c | 7c | 8c | 9c | 10c |
| Knowledge about language | | | | 6e | | 8e | 9e | 10e |
| Library and reference | | 4d | 5d | 6d | 7d | 8d | 9d | 10d |
| Use inference and deduction | 3c | 4c | 5b | 6b | | | | |
| Understand how stories are structured | 3e | | | | | | | |
| Understand literary devices and writers' use of language | | | 5e | 6e | 7e | 8b | 9b | 10b |

**EN3 WRITING**

| Write structured stories | 3c | 4b | | | | | | |
|---|---|---|---|---|---|---|---|---|
| Organise writing: punctuation, sentences, paragraphs | 3a | 4a | 5b | 6b | 7b | 8b | 9b | 10b |
| Write for different purposes and audiences | | | 5a | 6a | 7a | 8a | 9a | 10a |
| Drafting | 3e | 4e | 5d | 6d | 7d | | | |
| Recognise the difference between spoken and written language | | | | 6e | 7e | 8d | 9d | 10d |
| Use written and Standard English | | 4d | 5c | 6c | 7c | 8c | 9c | 10c |
| Write with an awareness of style | | | | 6c | | | | 10c |
| Produce non-chronological writing | 3d | 4c | 5a | 6a | 7a | 8a | 9a | 10a |

## APPENDIX B

### PUPIL RECORD FOR ENGLISH

Name ...................... Form ....... Teacher ..............

| Column 1 = Always true  2 = Normally true  3 = Not true | Term 1 | | | Term 2 | | | Term 3 | | |
|---|---|---|---|---|---|---|---|---|---|
| | 1 | 2 | 3 | 1 | 2 | 3 | 1 | 2 | 3 |
| **READING** | | | | | | | | | |
| I can read regularly at home | | | | | | | | | |
| I can read aloud without difficulty | | | | | | | | | |
| I read better in silence | | | | | | | | | |
| I can pick out the main points of what I have read | | | | | | | | | |
| I can talk about what I have read | | | | | | | | | |
| **WRITING** | | | | | | | | | |
| I can write my ideas clearly | | | | | | | | | |
| I can write about many subjects | | | | | | | | | |
| I find it easier to write stories | | | | | | | | | |
| I have good ideas | | | | | | | | | |
| I am good at describing things | | | | | | | | | |
| I can use my imagination | | | | | | | | | |
| I can plan my ideas | | | | | | | | | |
| I can do drafts of my work | | | | | | | | | |
| I can use full stops properly | | | | | | | | | |
| I can use commas properly | | | | | | | | | |
| I know when to use capital letters | | | | | | | | | |
| I can use the apostrophe properly | | | | | | | | | |
| I can use speech marks properly | | | | | | | | | |
| I can write in sentences | | | | | | | | | |
| I can write in paragraphs | | | | | | | | | |
| **SPEAKING AND LISTENING** | | | | | | | | | |
| I listen to my teacher | | | | | | | | | |
| I listen to others in my group | | | | | | | | | |
| I am good in group work | | | | | | | | | |
| I can explain things clearly | | | | | | | | | |
| I can ask and answer questions | | | | | | | | | |
| I can tell a story | | | | | | | | | |
| I have a lot to say | | | | | | | | | |
| **SPELLING** | | | | | | | | | |
| I can spell words that I want to use | | | | | | | | | |
| I don't get words confused (e.g. too/to) | | | | | | | | | |
| I check my own spelling | | | | | | | | | |
| **HANDWRITING** | | | | | | | | | |
| My handwriting is neat and clear | | | | | | | | | |
| I think others can read my writing | | | | | | | | | |
| **INFORMATION TECHNOLOGY** | | | | | | | | | |
| I use a word processor when allowed | | | | | | | | | |
| I use the library computerised catalogue | | | | | | | | | |
| I use CD-ROM to find information | | | | | | | | | |
| I can explain verbally how I used the computer | | | | | | | | | |
| I can write down how I used the computer | | | | | | | | | |

| | |
|---|---|
| What I enjoyed most this term was | **FIRST TERM** |

What I did best this term was

What I found most difficult was

What I have learned is

What I can try to improve is

| | |
|---|---|
| What I enjoyed most this term was | **SECOND TERM** |

What I did best this term was

What I found most difficult was

What I have learned is

What I can try to improve is

| | |
|---|---|
| What I enjoyed most this term was | **THIRD TERM** |

What I did best this term was

What I found most difficult was

What I have learned is

What I can try to improve is

NEWLAND SCHOOL   NATIONAL CURRICULUM ENGLISH ASSESSMENT RECORD   KEY STAGE 3 ATTAINMENT TARGETS

Name . . . . . . . . . . . . . . . . . . . . . . . .   Form . . . . . . . . . . . . .   Teacher . . . . . . . . . . . . . . . . . . .

| | | | | | | | | |
|---|---|---|---|---|---|---|---|---|
| **SPEAKING AND LISTENING (EN1)** | | | | | | | | |
| COMMUNICATION | | | | | | | | |
| LISTENING AND RESPONDING | | | | | | | | |
| **READING (EN2)** | | | | | | | | |
| INITIAL READING SKILLS | | | | | | | | |
| READING ALOUD | | | | | | | | |
| READING FOR INFORMATION | | | | | | | | |
| COMPREHENSION/UNDERSTANDING | | | | | | | | |
| CRITICAL READING (e.g. for bias) | | | | | | | | |
| APPRECIATION OF LITERATURE | | | | | | | | |
| KNOWLEDGE ABOUT LANGUAGE | | | | | | | | |
| **WRITING (EN3)** | | | | | | | | |
| PERSONAL WRITING (e.g. autobiography) | | | | | | | | |
| DESCRIPTIVE/IMAGINATIVE WRITING | | | | | | | | |
| NARRATIVE WRITING | | | | | | | | |
| EXPLANATORY WRITING | | | | | | | | |
| FACTUAL WRITING | | | | | | | | |
| ORGANISATIONAL WRITING (e.g. punctuation, sentence, paragraph) | | | | | | | | |
| DRAFTING | | | | | | | | |
| **SPELLING (EN4)** | | | | | | | | |
| **PRESENTATION (EN4/5)** | | | | | | | | |
| **HANDWRITING (EN5)** | | | | | | | | |
| DATE | | | | | | | | |

SPEAKING AND LISTENING

ASSIGNMENT
TEACHER'S COMMENTS

ASSIGNMENT
TEACHER'S COMMENTS

ASSIGNMENT
TEACHER'S COMMENTS

ASSIGNMENT
TEACHER'S COMMENTS

ASSIGNMENT
TEACHER'S COMMENTS

ASSIGNMENT
TEACHER'S COMMENTS

# APPENDIX C

**NEWLAND SCHOOL FOR GIRLS**
**FACULTY OF ENGLISH**
**PLANNING SHEET**

**TEACHER**

**CLASS**

**UNIT OF WORK**

**Date** . . . . . . . . **Signature** . . . . . . . . . . . . . . . . . . . . . . . . . . . . . . . . . . . . . . . . . .

| SPEAKING AND LISTENING (EN1) | READING (EN2) | WRITING (EN3) |
| --- | --- | --- |
| | | |

# KS 3/KS 4 ENGLISH ENTITLEMENTS

## EN1 SPEAKING AND LISTENING
- [ ] Improvise and take part in a role play
- [ ] Present/perform
- [ ] Interview/question
- [ ] Share personal experiences
- [ ] Explore ideas through talk
- [ ] Contribute and respond in group discussion
- [ ] Discuss facts and opinions
- [ ] Report and summarise
- [ ] Work in a variety of groupings
- [ ] Argue a point of view
- [ ] Use a tape recorder
- [ ] Tell a story/listen to a story
- [ ] Give and receive explanations and information
- [ ] Work with drama scripts

## EN3 WRITING
- [ ] Plan/brainstorm/take notes/make notes
- [ ] Write stories
- [ ] Diaries
- [ ] Letters
- [ ] Reviews and reports
- [ ] Surveys/questionnaire
- [ ] Write for different purposes and audiences
- [ ] Write poetry
- [ ] Write playscripts
- [ ] Summarise in writing
- [ ] Give an opinion in writing
- [ ] Structure an argument
- [ ] Write newspaper entries and brochures
- [ ] Illustrate and display work
- [ ] Write about fictional characters
- [ ] Write creatively in response to literature
- [ ] Write collaboratively
- [ ] Write to develop style
- [ ] Draft/redraft
- [ ] Spelling
- [ ] Punctuation
- [ ] Sentences
- [ ] Paragraphs

## CROSS-CURRICULAR THEMES
- [ ] Environment
- [ ] Health education
- [ ] Citizenship
- [ ] EIU
- [ ] Careers

## SCHOOL MANAGEMENT PLAN
- [ ] IT
- [ ] PSE
- [ ] Teaching/learning styles
- [ ] Equal opportunities

## EN2 READING
- [ ] Class novel/shared novel
- [ ] Small-group reading
- [ ] Individual reading book
- [ ] Sustained silent reading
- [ ] Read aloud
- [ ] Short stories
- [ ] Playscripts
- [ ] Letters
- [ ] Autobiographical writing
- [ ] Pre-twentieth-century texts
- [ ] Non-fiction/information/reference
- [ ] Newspapers/pamphlets/brochures
- [ ] Articles
- [ ] Comprehension and critical reading

## WORK CONTEXTS
- [ ] Individual
- [ ] Pair
- [ ] Small group
- [ ] Whole-class group
- [ ] Word processing/IT
- [ ] Library skills
- [ ] CD-ROM search
- [ ] Dictionary
- [ ] Thesaurus
- [ ] Reference
- [ ] Communicating with a wider audience
- [ ] SAT-related work
- [ ] GCSE/KS4 revision
- [ ] GCSE/KS4 coursework

## FACULTY MANAGEMENT PLAN
- [ ] National Curriculum
- [ ] Promote reading
- [ ] Differentiated work
- [ ] Drama links
- [ ] Display/classroom environment
- [ ] Whole-school politics
- [ ] AV
- [ ] IT

## CROSS-CURRICULAR SKILLS
- [ ] Communication
- [ ] Number
- [ ] Problem solving
- [ ] Information handling
- [ ] Practical
- [ ] PSE

# Chapter 7

# How do we teach grammar?

*Jane Lodge and Paul Evans*

## A BRIEF LOOK AT THE BACKGROUND

The subject of 'grammar' is a controversial one. There seems to be no general agreement even about what it is, which is the reason why we shall confine the word within inverted commas until we have defined it, at least to our own satisfaction. Further controversies have surrounded the questions of whether 'grammar' – whatever it is – should be taught at all; how it should be taught; which parts of it should be taught to children and at what age they should be taught it.

We do not intend to use the space allocated to us here to pick apart the strands of these controversies, but we would like to look back briefly at the history of the 'grammar' debate since 1984.

We choose 1984 as our starting point because it was in that year that the Department of Education and Science published the first document in an HMI series called 'Curriculum Matters' (DES, 1984). The document itself was called *English from 5 to 16*, and proposed objectives to be achieved by 7-, 11- and 16-year-olds. Included in the objectives for 11-year-olds, under the heading 'About language' was the following list (pp 8 and 9):

They should know:

- The rules of spelling
- The difference between vowels and consonants
- The function and names of the main parts of speech (noun, pronoun, verb, adjective and adverb), and be able to identify these in their own writing for the purpose of discussing what they have written
- The difference between statements, questions, commands and exclamations
- The terms 'subject' and 'object' and be able to identify them in their own writing
- That a sentence has a subject and a verb, and that the two must agree
- That word order determines meaning.

They should:

- Be aware of differences between tenses, and recognise when the past, present, or future tense is being used
- Know that language can be literal or figurative, and be aware of the difference when they use or respond to language.
- Be aware of some of the ways in which written language differs from spoken language.

The document invited responses, and incorporated reaction to those responses in the second edition of *English from 5 to 16* which appeared in 1986 (DES, 1986). In reporting on the responses which had been received, the second edition stated that 'Nothing divided the respondents more than the issue of knowledge about language' (p. 39, para 37) and noted 'the widespread and vigorous rejection of grammatical analysis and of teaching the terminology listed in the objectives' (p. 40, para 39).

In the appendix to the second edition, under the heading 'Objectives for English', we find the words (p. 44): 'What follows is a selection of illustrative examples of how, taking account of the reasoned responses to the original document, the objectives for the teaching of English might be recast.' Searching below for the recast equivalent of the section 'About language' in the original 1984 edition, we find that such a section no longer exists, but seems to have been replaced by two sentences (p. 48): 'Most pupils should also have progressed in their grasp of spelling, punctuation and the use of appropriate vocabulary. For most pupils simple proof-reading and editing should have become more habitual and have developed towards a greater self-sufficiency.'

It would be possible to spend a great deal of time analysing the significance of these quotations. We seek to demonstrate here that this relaunch into the educational debate of the 'grammar' question was marked by confusion, poor writing and hasty retreat. It should be some consolation to confused teachers to know that at least they are not as confused as HMI seems to have been in 1984 and 1986.

The task of defining the objectives for the teaching of English language was taken out of the hands of HMI and given to the Kingman Committee in 1988 (DES, 1988). In drawing up attainment targets for 7-, 11- and 16-year-olds, the committee made a distinction between 'aspects of pupil performance' and 'aspects of language upon which pupils should be expected to reflect and comment in the light of knowledge about language' (p. 52). Thus, to take one example from the attainment targets for 11-year-olds (p. 54), the pupil performance column reads: 'Write clearly enough to enable a reader to understand what is being referred to, either elsewhere in the text or in the outside world.' The pupil reflection column requires the pupil to: 'Understand how a text is made coherent by clear "referring expressions", consistent use of tenses, consistent style (e.g. in choice of vocabulary), as well as by conjunctions and punctuation which mark the relationship between what is said now with what has been said already, and what is to follow.'

The Kingman Report represents a move away from the prescription of the HMI document. It makes a distinction between explicit performance criteria and rather more implicit understandings which teachers should seek to develop in their pupils. It advocates that these understandings should be encouraged through reflection, rather than taught by prescription. When it comes, however, to expressing what these understandings might be, the language of the report becomes opaque and, dare we say, un-grammatical. (We refer the reader back to the last quotation in the previous paragraph.) It is difficult to be clear and concise in these matters.

In the Cox Report of 1989 (DES/WO, 1989), which formed the basis of the Statutory Orders for National Curriculum English, the notions of implicit understanding and learning through reflection were retained, codified into the required ten levels and expressed, by and large, in clear language. Thus, at level 4 in the Attainment Target for Writing, pupils are required to (17.34): 'show some competence in the structures of written Standard English and begin to use some sentence structures different from those which are characteristic of speech, eg a wider range of subord-inate clauses, expanded noun phrases etc.' and to: 'attempt independent redrafting and revision of their own writing and talk about changes they have made'. Now the objectives are expressed in a language which is accessible to teachers, and perhaps to parents; it points the way towards a language in which these issues may be tackled by pupils. The Cox Report remains, in our view, the most coherent of these statements about language, and we shall return to it later.

The Language in the National Curriculum (LINC) project ran from 1989 to 1992 (LINC, 1989–92). It was funded by the Department of Edu-cation and Science and by the local education authorities of England and Wales. Its specific aim was to acquaint teachers with the model of lan-guage presented in the Kingman Report. The training, it is claimed, involved teachers in every school in England and Wales. The govern-ment, however, was unhappy with the materials which the LINC project produced. At first, the government insisted that the materials should be used for teacher training purposes only. Later, it banned their publication altogether, and the materials now exist only as samizdat photocopies around the country. Obviously, the subject is no less controversial now than it has been throughout the past thirty years. We can only guess at the reasons for the project's unpopularity with the government. LINC handed back to teachers and educationalists the prime responsibility to consider how the English language should be taught. It went beyond its brief of publicising the Kingman model. It generated huge amounts of material, of a fairly complex nature, and a large degree of enthusiasm in the teaching profession.

In 1993 there appeared a draft proposal for the revision of the Statutory Orders in English (DFE, 1993). In its prescriptive tone, it most resembled the HMI proposals with which we began. All mention of the notion of knowledge about language had been removed from it. It seemed destined to receive an unfavourable response from most educationalists, but was almost immediately sidelined by the announcement of a full review of the National Curriculum by Sir Ron Dearing.

At the time of writing, we have before us the new draft proposals for National Curriculum English (SCAA, 1994). The draft seems to us to be a cunningly constructed work, designed both to placate political masters and to allow English teachers sufficient latitude to follow their own well-documented convictions. Prominence is given to the notion of Standard English, though nowhere is it explicitly defined. If one looks carefully enough, one can still find sentences and phrases which would permit teachers to welcome and to develop their pupils' own under-standings about language: 'Their study of language should relate to their reading and their previous linguistic experience, written and oral' (p. 27, 3.1). The proposal is bland and bureaucratic in tone. It does not inspire enthusiasm. We can live with it.

## THE VIEW FROM THE CLASSROOM

What should the practising teacher do, faced both with the evidence of this confused, often polarised debate and with classes of children waiting to be taught?

Our answer is: Hold true to your own philosophy of teaching, be absolutely clear about your objectives and strategies and always keep yourself informed and open to change.

We have found this a very difficult chapter to write. We have been forced to examine both our philosophy and our practice, to define our terms every step of the way and to take account of different approaches towards 'grammar'. The process of thinking this matter through has proved to be invigorating and re-energising. That is what 'grammar' has done for us. We believe that, tackled in the same spirit in classrooms, it can do the same for other teachers and for pupils.

Between us, we have over thirty years of classroom experience, in primary, middle and secondary schools. Over that period of time, we have evolved a philosophy of teaching and a strategy for delivering that philosophy. We believe that most teachers will do exactly the same thing over the course of their careers, and that it is unreasonable, and un-productive, to ask teachers to teach in a way which goes against their convictions. On the other hand, the notion of flexibility is an important feature of many teachers' philosophies. Many teachers would feel it important to be open to new learning experiences, to be willing to modify or change their views. And so we have questioned our own responses to the notion of 'grammar' in preparing this piece of writing, and we invite our readers to do the same.

In this chapter, we will put the teaching of 'grammar' within the framework of our philosophy of teaching.

We aim to provide answers to such questions as:

- What is 'grammar'?
- How should teachers go about fulfilling National Curriculum obligations in this area?
- How does meeting these obligations fit into current best practice?
- Can 'grammar' be taught in a mixed-ability classroom?
- Does the pupil have an active part to play in this process?

Finally, we will provide detailed examples which show how we put our philosophy into practice in our classrooms.

## WHAT IS OUR PHILOSOPHY?

English is the study of the language and its literature. Our aims as English teachers are to improve pupils' understanding about how the English language works, to explore with them the uses to which speakers and writers have put the language and to help them to become more effective in their use of the language.

We want our pupils to be active participants in our lessons: when we, as teachers, have knowledge to impart, we want our pupils actively to engage with it rather than to receive it passively. We believe that it is important to make explicit to pupils the nature of what they are studying, so that they know not only what they are doing but also why they are doing it. We want to eliminate, as far as is possible, any 'hidden agenda' on the part of teachers. We recognise the need for a degree of negotiation in the exchange between teacher and pupil. We seek the transfer of a degree of responsibility for the framing and completion of the task from teacher to pupil.

We believe that the elements of our philosophy which we have listed above can be traced in all the National Curriculum documents now in force. We were delighted to find confirmation of this view from Peter Latham (Latham, 1992) who has argued that there are four assumptions about learning which underpin the National Curriculum in all its published documents and across all the key stages. These assumptions, in paraphrase, are:

- that learning is most likely to be effective when learners are active in formulating their own questions and developing their own strategies for problem solving;

- that teachers need to acknowledge and use what learners already know, as a basis for extending their learning;
- that reflection has to be an essential aspect of learning, helping to make explicit to learners what they know;
- that learning is fundamentally a social and collaborative enterprise.

Our philosophy informs all our teaching, including our work in the controversial area of 'grammar'. Those teachers interested in developing a cross-curricular approach to learning might also find, as we have, that these assumptions about learning provide a starting point for investigation within their own schools.

## WHAT IS OUR STRATEGY?

We have found the following strategy to be very helpful in making the process of learning explicit to pupils. It needs to be explained at this point in order to make clear the framework in which our work on 'grammar' takes place. The strategy is called 'Plan–Do–Review', and can be explained briefly as follows:

| PLAN |
| --- |
| Teachers are clear in their own minds about the nature and purpose of the tasks they set. The task may be designed to allow pupils to demonstrate understanding of particular elements of the National Curriculum, or it may have broader aims. It does not, however, have vague ones. Assessment can only be effective when it is carried out against criteria which have been defined and understood at the time the task was set. |
| Pupils know not only what they are doing, but why they are doing it. They are taken into the planning process, playing a part in planning their own tasks when appropriate. |

| DO |
| --- |
| Teachers do a great deal of assessment, both of talk and of writing, during lessons. They realise the significance of talk at the moment it is spoken. They are able to look at a piece of writing and suggest a way to develop it. They seize upon and improvise opportunities for |

> teaching and learning, based upon their clear understanding of the nature of the task, which they share with the pupils.

> Pupils work in a variety of groupings, so that they are able fully to develop and demonstrate their abilities and understandings. They are given opportunities to choose ways in which to carry their work forward.

## REVIEW

> Teachers assess on the basis of the criteria which they set out at the beginning of the task. They assess in a variety of formal and informal ways. They take pupils into the assessment process, because they see the process as a prime agent for cognitive and social growth.

> Pupils are given the opportunity, through the widest variety of means, to express their knowledge and understanding, and to reflect on their own performance and that of others.

## WHAT IS GRAMMAR?

Now it is time to take the inverted commas away from the word grammar, and to arrive at a working definition of the term.

At this point we must acknowledge our indebtedness to Chapters Four, Five and Six of the Cox Report.

We were interested to see that Chapter Five: 'Linguistic Terminology' begins with this quotation from Jerome Bruner: 'The cultivation of reflectiveness, or whatever you choose to call it, is one of the great problems one faces in devising curriculum.'

Reflectiveness (or review, as we have called it in describing our strategy) is seen by Cox to be the key to the question of when and how to introduce linguistic terminology into the classroom. When pupils begin to look closely at what they have written or said, it is the right moment to help them towards the concepts and vocabulary they need to develop their work. This notion clearly fits in with our philosophy and leads into a definition of grammar which is wide rather than narrow.

The quotation from Bruner is also apt in its emphasis on the fact that encouraging pupils to be reflective is problematic. To what extent should their reflectiveness be guided by the teacher in a direction which the teacher feels to be productive? Having given the pupils permission to be reflective, the teacher now faces the problems of how and where to draw the line. How much time can be spent on reflection rather than on the production of new material? We hope to show how we tackle these issues when we give examples of our classroom practice.

We reject, as Cox does, the narrow definition of grammar as the analysis of parts of speech and sentence structure (5.20). In our view, this definition is too restrictive and is likely to encourage the bad practice of teaching 'grammar exercises', which are divorced from any context that has meaning for the pupil.

The wider definition, which we endorse, is that grammar is the systematic discussion of language in use. It includes consideration of the following issues (5.20–26):

- the changes in language to suit form, audience and purpose;
- the different effects which can be achieved in speech and writing;
- the reasons why some language structures are ambiguous or misleading;
- the study of elements larger than sentences;
- the introduction of specialist terminology in context, for a purpose.

Within this definition, there are balances which must be struck by each teacher, judgements which must be made over and over again in the light of changing circumstances in the classroom. To what extent can grammatical knowledge be left implicit? How and when should it be made explicit? What does the teacher need to know about grammar? How prescriptive should the teacher be? What do the pupils need to know in any given situation? What do all pupils need to know? What should be available for those pupils who choose to learn more? All these questions need to be considered when a teacher plans a series of lessons, and they need to be firmly in the teacher's mind when decisions have to be made quickly during actual lessons. A teacher's specific answers to these questions, then, will vary as much as classroom circumstances vary. The illustrative examples which follow will, we hope, show how we answered these questions in two specific, and very different, situations.

The 1995 English Orders have turned out to be less prescriptive with regard to grammar than might have been expected after the 1994 Draft Proposals. Nevertheless, teachers still have to decide how to balance the obligation to deliver the National Curriculum against the need to be true to what they feel is appropriate for their pupils. We believe that it is possible to deliver what the government requires and to go a step further, teaching in an imaginative and exploratory manner.

Exploration is a very tricky business. As a demonstration of how difficult it is to say anything at once clear and accurate about grammar, consider the remarks of William Cobbett which are quoted at the beginning of Chapter Six of the Cox Report: 'Grammar, perfectly understood, enables us, not only to express our meaning fully and clearly, but so to express it as to defy the ingenuity of man to give to our words any other meaning than that which we ourselves intend them to express.'

Even William Cobbett has surely not got it quite right. It is in the course of the struggle to say something that we become clearer about what it is we wish to say: we may even discover thoughts inside our heads which we did not know existed. Equally, our readers may well have thoughts which we had not anticipated, and they may thus put upon our words constructions which we never imagined. It is these elements of surprise and uncertainty within the struggle for self-expression which make the arid sounding study of grammar potentially so stimulating.

## TWO ILLUSTRATIVE EXAMPLES

We take one of our examples from our teaching of a creative writing task, with Year 7 pupils, and the other from the teaching of an analytical writing task, with Year 10 pupils.

These tasks could be seen to some extent as generic, since the approach which we illustrate here is intended to represent many of the features of our teaching in general. In writing these accounts, we have, of course, emphasised those elements of the lessons which deal directly with grammar, as we have defined it. It must be said that, on analysis, we found that grammar was a central concern of these tasks.

We aim to show that:

- the active involvement of the pupils is important at every stage of the work;
- pupils consider both the characteristics of an established author's writing and those of their own work;
- drafting, proof-reading and editing are essential elements in the investigation of grammar;
- the balance between pupils' implicit and explicit knowledge about language is an ever present consideration in the teacher's mind;
- existing and possible future National Curriculum obligations are addressed;
- these activities are appropriate in a mixed-ability classroom.

### Creative writing with Year 7

We wanted the pupils to complete a piece of atmospheric 'horror' writing. We chose this theme because it seems to interest almost everybody and almost invariably leads to a high level of success. We also wanted to enhance the pupils' explicit understanding of how such writing is achieved. This is, therefore, a task very much concerned with grammar, as we have defined it.

We began by explaining the task to the pupils so that they were aware from the start of the reason for exploring the models of writing. One of the models we used was a short story called 'The Ghost', by Catherine Wells (9). A girl is confined to bed in a large house due to illness and is waiting for a friend to dress up as a ghost in order to frighten her. In fact she sees a 'real' ghost. Thinking that it is her friend, she is not alarmed, until the end of the story when the friend knocks on the door and says, 'I'm ready now. Shall I begin?' The reader is left in no doubt as to the reality of the ghost because of the way in which the writing builds up tension.

We asked the pupils to imagine themselves in a similar situation and to jot down the central facts: where they were; why they were in bed; what time of day it was, and so on.

In a teacher-led session, we then began to draw up a table to explore the way in which Catherine Wells had made us feel a little uneasy. The teacher introduced the first example of a way in which an atmosphere of fear had been created in the story. The pupils then found more examples and commented on them. As always, the pupils found more techniques than the teacher had anticipated. There was a great deal of interest in this activity, as many pupils were already deciding which techniques they would use in their own writing. The less able pupils spent longer finding their own examples and consequently ended the lesson with a shorter list of techniques. This made the next stage easier for them, since they had fewer techniques to choose from when they came to their own writing.

We ended with the following as a complete list of the techniques, parts of speech and punctuation marks which the pupils felt were used to create the sense of tension in the story:

sounds described in detail;
short sentences;
commas;
paragraphs;
adjectives;
verbs;
questions;
hyphens;
dots.

Pupils then attempted to write a paragraph, using adjectives to build an atmosphere of horror.

We read and enjoyed these, with teacher and pupils pointing out good examples. Next we read 'Fever Dream' by Ray Bradbury[1] and applied the same method of analysis to it. The pupils were able to find many examples and this increased their confidence.

In quoting pupils' work, the only corrections which we have made are to the spelling. Here is an example of a technique table, showing one pupil's comments:

| How fear is created | Examples |
|---|---|
| Questions make the reader want to answer them. It encourages them to read farther. | 'The lamp flame gave a sudden fitful leap. Why? Was it going out? Was it? – no.' |
| Short sentences. Every time a full stop is put in, it makes a pause which often creates a silence. | 'He could never come through that? It must have yawned open of its own accord.' |
| This paragraph shows how commas can change a piece of writing. They make the speed change. This makes the reader all tight and by the end of the paragraph you can imagine the scene. | 'Her heart began to beat rather quickly. She could see only the upper part of the door, the foot of her bed hid the lower third . . .' |

Here is an example of a pupil's writing, where she has stated the techniques she intends to use and completed her first draft.

I am going to use adjectives to set the scene, short sentences to be like scared breaths and paragraphs to show where the girl is reading from her book.

### Horror At Hemming Hill

She woke up suddenly. She looked around, aroused by the creaking tree outside her window. The dark, black, blanket sky was cold in the mid October wind. The open window let the breeze into her pokey bedroom, swishing the curtains. The surroundings were more clear now, she could see the bookcase and the table. She lit a match and turned on the light. It gave a slight flicker and went onto full glow. The room looked so different in the warm, mellow glow. The fire was still alight, just. She went over and gave it a poke. The yellow, orange flames were soon licking the chimney. She took a book off the bookcase, blew off the cobwebs and went back into the big, cast iron bed. It creaked. She opened the first page and straightened it out.

Jill was nine and had flu. She lived at Hemming Hill Castle in the room facing East.

She froze with utter shock. It was the same room that she was in now! She turned to the cover and discovered that Margaret Hemming was the author. Auntie Maggie! She turned back to the book.

As Jill got used to the room she began to realise that things were moving. At first it was just hairbrushes and combs but as time went on it began to be chairs and tables. Jill was always getting shouted at for leaving things around

Elizabeth was sure it was the room she was in. Who was Jill? Was she a relation? She turned back to her book.

The next morning it was worse, mirrors smashed, ornaments shattered all over the hard floor. Jill climbed out of the bed to tidy up the mess suddenly, out of the blue a hand pulled around her neck forcing her to collapse onto the shattered glass and ornaments. The next morning she was dead strangled.

The end

Elizabeth, shocked and shaking went to turn off the light, when she felt a cold, arctic, rigid hand, placed on her shaking shoulder.

But who was doing this? She turned. She felt an icy hand on her stiff shoulder. She turned. She turned to face this monstrous creature lurking in the mist of her bedroom. She felt his hard, cold teeth plunge into her frail neck, exhausted she fell to the floor. Dead.

The end

After writing the first draft, pupils worked in pairs to correct sentence structure, spelling and, where necessary, to improve on their use of the techniques they had chosen. We asked the pairs to identify a sentence which seemed in some way wrong to them and to try to put it right. If they could not, they asked for help. We then offered suggestions and the pupils tried again. Pupils had the use of a dictionary and a thesaurus when correcting and improving work.

Finally, here is an example of the finished product, as it was written up for display.

---

### SUDDENLY

I can hear footsteps on the roof, the wind is howling and blowing the dressing gown up and lurking around the door. The slippers seem to be moving. Everywhere I look there's something horrifying wrong. My bed is cold, my feet have gone numb.

I know there's something wrong in this old house but I daren't get up because I don't know what's down there. The walls seem to be cracking and as though any minute there's going to be a terrifying thing that I'll always regret.

Suddenly the door knob moved. The brown door was moving. I was moving as well, towards it. My heart stopped beating for a second. There stood behind the door was something but I couldn't see it, but I could hear footsteps going under the bed and towards the white slippers.

It slithered. I knew there was something there but I couldn't see anything. There was a loudish cry coming from the downstairs in the washer room. I carefully went down the stairs, but they had a weird feeling to them. It was as though people were trying to grab my feet, so I flew down them. My whole body was in shock and overcoming the fear, I went through the kitchen and my footsteps gradually got slower and slower until I stopped. All the clothes in the washing machine were all over the cold stone floor but I still didn't know what was causing this. I looked all around but nothing. I started to clear the clothes away and suddenly . . . .

The next day Jenny was stone cold and in the back of her neck were three teeth marks but not even the doctor that took the post mortem could not even find out what killed her. So it was a mystery how Jenny Mellor died. The funeral was carried out on 13th September and everyone was very upset. The family was never the same after Jenny Mellor died, on that terrible day.

---

### Analytical writing with Year 10

The nature of the task is simply stated: to write an essay on the Philip Larkin poem 'The Old Fools'.[2] Simple to state; hard to deliver.

We devised the task as an introduction to the GCSE course at the start of Year 10. We wanted to use a poem, since the study of poetry inevitably involves the detailed study of language. We wanted to put before the pupils a stimulus which would stir them up a bit, even shock them perhaps. Larkin's view of old age is probably not one which they have heard expressed so forcefully in anything they have read earlier. Although they might well have written about old people themselves in previous tasks, it would probably not have been in such terms. There was certainly a reaction from the pupils on first hearing Larkin's description of the old 'pissing themselves'!

So, we wanted something which had impact. We also wanted something which had depth, which was difficult to understand, which would repay close attention. But we did not want a piece which would be off-putting because of its length. Although this poem is difficult, everyone stands a chance of getting to grips with it because it is short.

The choice of this poem also seemed appropriate for a mixed-ability group. There is language which has an immediate impact and can be analysed at the level of the concrete, such as the descriptions of 'ash hair, toad hands, prune face dried into lines'. But there are also changes in mood, tone and vocabulary which will allow pupils to chart the changes, describe them and attempt to account for them.

We also considered the question of presenting the pupils with a model for their writing. We thought of good essayists – Hazlitt, Orwell – but realised that this was not really the kind of model we had in mind for the essay we wanted our pupils to write. The model we were working to, almost subconsciously until we thought about it clearly, is the kind of essay required by the GCSE examination boards. Did we, then, want to put before our pupils examples of essays written by previous examinees? We decided that we did not, principally because we did not want, at this early stage, to run the risk that the pupils would feel that their ideas were acceptable only if they were packaged in a specific way. This decision does, of course, raise the issue, previously mentioned, of 'hidden agenda'. We, the teachers, knew what we were aiming at; they, the pupils, did not. How we tackled this problem in the classroom will be revealed shortly.

What actually happened in the classroom? We read the poem aloud to the pupils several times, telling them that they would have to write about it in a few minutes' time. We also played a cassette recording of Larkin himself reading the poem. Then we asked the pupils to write down their reactions to the poem. We emphasised that we wanted an individual response: they were not to talk to each other at this stage, or to read what anyone else was writing. We told them that nothing they wrote could possibly be wrong, as long as it was related to the poem. We asked them to write as much as possible, to keep writing until we asked them to stop, to let their thoughts flow onto the paper. At this point, we relented in our quest to secure their thoughts completely unadulterated by outside influences, because we felt that some pupils could well be feeling uneasy about being left entirely on their own in a situation which was possibly unfamiliar to them. We suggested, then, that, if they wished, they could answer some of the questions which we were now about to ask. While they wrote, we asked such questions as: What do you think Larkin's attitude towards old people is? Do you agree with his attitude? What do you think about the way he talks about them? Why do you think he writes about them in this way? Where is he imagining them living? What is he imagining them doing? If you get stuck for something to write, pick out a few words of the poem and write about them.

After they had worked on this for about fifteen minutes, we asked them to close their books and tell the person sitting next to them what they had written. Then, as the first lesson was drawing to a close, we gave them the following essay plan.

---

Write a critical appreciation of the poem 'The Old Fools' by Philip Larkin.
Try to follow this plan:

Part 1: The subject of the poem
      a)   What is the poem about?
      b)   What is the tone of the poem?
      c)   What is the poet's attitude towards his subject?
      d)   What are his intentions in writing the poem?

Part 2: The form and style of the poem
      a)   What is the structure of the poem?
      b)   How would you describe the language of the poem?
      c)   What images does the poet use?

Part 3: An evaluation of the poem
      a)   Do the form and style of the poem help the poet to achieve his intentions (see 1d)?
      b)   Do you think the poem is a success?
      c)   What were your reactions to the poem?

---

We asked them to go home and make an attempt at any part of the essay they wished, except Part 3c, which we felt they would probably have covered sufficiently, for the time being, in their first spontaneous response.

At the start of the next lesson, we asked them to work with a friend as a response partner, using the following guidelines:

## WORKING WITH A RESPONSE PARTNER

Find out which part of the essay your partner has tackled.
Read through carefully what your partner has written.
Is the meaning of your partner's writing CLEAR?
Ask your partner to explain the meaning.
Help your partner to write more clearly.
Is there anything more that can be said on this subject?
Discuss the subject with your partner, and help your partner to
    write down any new points.
Is your partner's work written in sentences?
Is the rest of the punctuation accurate?
Is your partner's work written in paragraphs?
Is the spelling accurate?

What follows is an example of one pupil's work thus far. As before, the only change which we have made is the correction of spelling mistakes.

## 1. FIRST REACTIONS

I don't think this man really likes old people
I don't think I've ever saw any old person that sits with their mouth open and drooling but I have seen them on the telly.
I think Philip Larkin wrote this poem from his own experiences maybe he didn't have very nice grandparents or they had senile dementia.
I don't understand the first lines of the second verse because when you die you don't break up into bits.
I don't think some of the parts in the poem were all true.
On the tape Philip sounded like a very stern man and he didn't really have a Hull accent.
Not all old people give an air of baffledness like this man says.

## 2. ANSWERING THE QUESTION FROM THE ESSAY PLAN: WHAT IS THIS POEM ABOUT?

The poem is a view on old people, the way Philip Larkin sees them he said some strange things about them and some were sympathetic towards them.

---

**3. WORKING WITH A RESPONSE PARTNER ON THE SAME QUESTION**

The poem also means that old people are going back to childhood because they are losing control of their minds and they are slowly drifting away. And when they die they gradually go away from your memory you still remember them but not as good as when they were alive.

When he talks about oblivion and he says 'At death, you break up: the bits that were you start speeding away from each other forever with no one to see, it's only oblivion true we had it before, but it was going to end', when he says this I think he means when we die we go into oblivion and when he say's we've been here before it was when we were in our mothers stomach and when he says it had to end it was when we come out and was born.

I think he doesn't believe in life after death because he says 'Next time you can't pretend there'll be anything'.

---

At this point, we became more interventionist, in two ways. We directed the pupils' attention both to specific examples of the way in which Larkin uses language and to the language which they themselves were using to write about the poem.

In dealing with Larkin's use of language, we asked the pupils such questions as:

• What is the effect of the constant use of questions in the poem?
• What is the effect of the images, such as 'the million-petalled flower' and 'extinction's alp'?
• Why does Larkin use nouns as if they were adjectives, in the line 'ash hair, toad hands, prune face dried into lines –'?
• Why does Larkin alternate between the use of colloquial (a word which came from a pupil) and poetic language?

During this session, we aimed to provide or, in some cases, to draw out from pupils the necessary vocabulary to facilitate discussion – words and concepts such as 'imagery', 'tone', 'enjambment' and so on – without giving the pupils our own answers to the questions we were posing.

We also looked, in detail, at the language which they were using as they wrote. For example, we considered the summary, quoted above, which one pupil wrote in answer to the question: What is the poem about?

The class as a group identified four points which the writer was seeking to make:

- that the poem was about old people;
- that the poem represented Larkin's views on old people;
- that he had some strange things to say about them;
- that he was to some extent sympathetic towards them.

Each member of the class then tried to write an introductory sentence or two to their essay, aiming to set out clearly what the poem was about. We looked at some of the efforts.

> The poem means asking a question about who the old fools are, and what is slowly happening to their minds, all described in an interesting view

When discussing this example, many pupils were keen to talk about the punctuation, without stopping to make any judgement about the validity or the clarity of what was actually being said. There is a difficult message to get across here: that the search for the correct form cannot be divorced from the search for meaning. We talked, among other things, about what kind of questions these were that Larkin was asking, and about whether it means anything to say that his view is 'interesting'.

> The poem is about the way old people are. It is also about what they do. The poem is very hard on old people in some ways. The poem is also sympathetic towards old people in a way.

These sentences served to illustrate the point that, in the effort to be clear, there is a danger of being simplistic. We also sought to demonstrate from this example that it is possible to be both simple and vague.

We will end here the detailed account of the lessons. We hope it is evident that we are attempting to introduce our pupils to the complexities of analytical writing, in a way which does not shy away from the immensity of the task, and yet is sensitive to the ideas and the needs of individual pupils. The lessons continued. Pupils worked alone, in pairs, in groups and as a class. The teacher talked to individuals, pairs, groups and the whole class. Before boredom or frustration set in (we hope) we asked the pupils to produce a draft essay and, after further review, a final version.

The pupil whose three early efforts we quoted above began the final version of the essay thus:

> The poem 'The old fools' is about old people but through the eyes of Philip Larkin. Some things he says about them are very biased and cynical but other things are very sympathetic.
>
> The poem is about old people going back into childhood Because in verse 1 when he says about them pissing themselves and drooling, it is just like when they were little, they can't do anything for themselves. They are losing control of their minds and they are slowly drifting away.
>
> When Larkin talks about death in verse 2 and how we break up into bits I think he means that when we die all the things that made us us, an individual go away, our personality our attitude and all the things like that just go away, there isn't an us anymore there's just a dead body.

When they had completed the final version of the essay, the pupils were asked to consider how well they thought they had tackled the task. Here are the comments of two pupils:

> I faced some problems when writing the first version of the essay my main problem was that I put a sort of answer to most of the questions at the beginning of the essay so I had to keep repeating myself. I also tended to linger too long on one question and spent less time on others. I tried to make my final version a bit more compact and I tried to cut some parts out that weren't really necessary I think I could make my future essays a bit more compact and to the point and improve my handwriting.

> At first I didn't really understand the poem It took me over a week to understand the poem fully. (or what I thought the poem meant). I wrote a rough copy of the essay first. When I wrote that, I was finding it hard to complete 8 pages but in the final copy I changed things around, added more of what I thought and left out some of the things I didn't think was right any more because I had understood the poem more. And I overcome that problem and I managed to write 10 pages.

We hope that we have demonstrated clearly our view that the teaching of grammar should be regarded as an integral part of the everyday work of the English classroom. It is our aim that, through the activities of speaking, listening, reading and writing, planning, doing and reviewing, our pupils gain confidence in themselves as proficient and innovative users of the English language.

## REFERENCES AND FURTHER READING.

1. Bradbury, Ray (1976) 'Fever Dream' in *Escapades*, selected by John L Foster and Edward Arnold, London
2. Larkin, Philip (1974) 'The Old Fools' in *High Windows*, Faber and Faber, London

DES (1984) *English from 5 to 16*, Curriculum Matters 1, An HMI Series, HMSO
DES (1986) *English from 5 to 16, Second Edition (incorporating responses)*, HMSO
DES (1988) *Report of the Committee of Inquiry into the Teaching of English Language*, HMSO
DES/WO (1989) *English for Ages 5 to 16*, HMSO
DFE (1993) *English for Ages 5 to 16*, HMSO
DFE (1994) *English in the National Curriculum: Draft Proposals*, DFE, May
DFE (1995) *English in the National Cuuriculum*, HMSO
Latham, Peter (1992) 'Oracy in the National Curriculum', *Thinking Voices* (pp. 256–62), ed. Kate Norman, Hodder and Stoughton, London
LINC (1989–92) 'Language in the National Curriculum, materials for professional development', unpublished
SCAA (1994) *English in the National Curriculum: Draft Proposals (May 1994)*, Schools Curriculum & Assessment Authority

# Chapter 8

# How can we teach Shakespeare?

*John Haddon*

The challenge of the National Curriculum in regard to Shakespeare is twofold: How do we make Shakespeare accessible to *all* our pupils? And how do we avoid being dictated to by the framework of understanding that might be suggested by the programmes of study and public examinations, without disadvantaging our pupils?

In recent years there has been a wide range of practice in the teaching of Shakespeare in secondary schools, from 'traditional' methods with more academic classes bound for A-level and beyond, through a variety of more active and experimental approaches, to complete abstention. It is only this last option that has been removed by the requirements of the National Curriculum, which continue to follow the recommendation of the Cox Report that 'Every pupil should be given at least some experience of Shakespeare's plays'.[1] Behind Cox's recommendation was a recognition of the continuing power and potential of the plays, together with an awareness of the wide range of work that can be done using active methods with secondary age pupils (as shown by the investigations of the Shakespeare in Schools project[2]) and the range of varied understandings and valuations of Shakespeare in academic criticism over recent years. Both the project and the critics emphasise the variety of potential *performances* of Shakespeare, and work for the most part with an awareness that Shakespeare wrote plays, not books.

At odds with Cox's open view, which can be taken to encourage continued exploration and experiment, is the somewhat simplistic version of a 'cultural heritage' view presently favoured by some influential politicians. The tendency of this view, which appeared strongly in both the 1993 (NCC, 1993) and 1994 (SCAA, 1994) proposals for a rewritten National Curriculum in English, is to see the plays as *literature* in the sense of books with stable and approved meanings, to downgrade performance, and to favour a transmission model of teaching. This 'cultural heritage' view seems to lie behind the inclusion of Shakespeare in the 1993 SATs (there was and is no statutory requirement to *examine* knowledge of Shakespeare).

The SATs requirements were reduced and improved in the wake of the 1993 boycott and the Dearing Review. Although the revised tests remain to some extent artificial and questionable, it should be possible, with an appropriate approach, for our pupils to take them in their stride. If we have a conception of Shakespeare's work *across whole key stages*, then the written exam need only be viewed as one outcome among many – not even, from our point of view, the most important. We need to work with a sense of a *range* of possible outcomes, not the same for all our pupils, nor all within our vision or control. What we choose to value and to question in Shakespeare will vary with our convictions, but what is required is a way of approaching Shakespeare that is accessible (at first) to all our pupils, is capable of a variety of developments, allows achievement in the terms determined by the terminal exam and does all that can be done to permit and encourage other kinds of achievement, always remaining potentially open and honest.

In preparing work on Shakespeare across the key stages, we need a framework of understanding that will help us keep in mind various important aspects of Shakespeare's plays, areas in which our pupils may experience difficulty but in which they may also achieve a great deal in the way of understanding. Work on Shakespeare should involve, in varying degrees, a recognition of three interrelated elements:

1  a sense of the plays as *playtexts* (scripts in need of performance and interpretation) and of the *theatrical space* in which they are performed;
2  knowledge of and response to the *stories* of human action and feeling that the plays dramatise;
3  some grasp of the *language* in which the stories are dramatised.

These elements can only be separated up to a point in the following sections; as the exposition of each progresses more of the others are assumed. It should be said that the aim is to give notes that will help in thinking about the organisation of teaching, rather than to offer a developmental model.

## PLAYSCRIPT AND THEATRICAL SPACE

Children who approach the text of Shakespeare's plays should have already a clear grasp of what a playscript is. They should be aware of the ways in which the writer of a script can establish place, time, characters and situation, and of the differences between playscript and other kinds of writing. They can consider the roles of narrators, and conventions such as the aside and the soliloquy for the externalisation of thought or framing commentary. In working with Shakespeare's plays as scripts they will find how few stage directions there are, how many possibilities to be explored, how many decisions to be taken. And they can be told (it is worth knowing) that many of the stage directions are editorial. At times it will be appropriate to find the implicit stage directions: for instance, 'I see thee yet, in form as palpable / As this which now I draw' and 'Thus die I, thus, thus, thus' (must Pyramus stab himself four times?).

The interpretation of playscript demands a sense of *theatrical space*. It makes a difference where characters are standing, whom they speak to, where and when they move. And drama is quintessentially something that is *watched*. Pupils working on a scene often have to be asked: 'Where's the audience?' Without experience of the disposition of the action (including speech) in theatrical space, our sense of the plays remains limited. (A caveat is required here, however: when considering Shakespeare's plays as playtexts we should not neglect the sustained, considered *reading* to which they will answer and which should be one of the possibilities that we envisage for some of our pupils.)

In order to give a framework for thinking about theatrical space, it can be useful to introduce pupils to three basic types of stage and be helped to consider their advantages and disadvantages:

- the proscenium stage – separated from the audience behind a proscenium arch, with scenery on flats and flies and sets changeable behind curtains;
- the thrust stage – a platform thrusting out into the audience who sit on three sides; open to the audience at all times;
- the arena stage – 'in the round'; the audience surrounds the actors.

They can be given scenes and invited to decide (a) what type of stage would suit them best and why, (b) how they would arrange the staging. Different groups might be given the same scene but asked to work it out for different stages. In doing these exercises pupils should consider the relationship between actors and audience, asking such questions as 'What difference would it make if s/he delivered the speech from *here*, as if s/he was (or wasn't) taking the audience into his/her confidence?'

Experimenting with different organisations of playspace usefully *precedes* the giving of information about the Elizabethan stage, although some teachers will prefer (or feel that there is only time) to start with the stage for which Shakespeare actually wrote. Either way, what is important is to investigate the stage's potential by using whatever approximations to it we can provide. Of course it is not always easy to provide ourselves with a large area to use as playspace, but the classroom can be enough if pupils are used to the necessary furniture moving, and in good weather classes can be taken in the open air (which is after all where Shakespeare's plays were first produced). It is important that they get some impression of the nature and size of Shakespeare's stage and of the kinetic sense of the drama, but they do not have to work in that way all the time, and when space is unfriendly they can work with diagrams (perhaps sketching particular stage positions on a drawing of an Elizabethan stage).

Here is an example of a Year 9 worksheet on the sleepwalking scene from *Macbeth* that covers many of the points considered in this section:

---

Read these notes about Shakespearean stage:

> **A large wooden platform above ground level, with audience on three sides. Entrances through two doors at either side of the back wall of the stage. High on the back wall there is a gallery for actors and musicians, with a separate entrance. Below the gallery an 'inner stage' inset in the wall, that can be covered by drawing a curtain. No scenery other than props. Open-air. No special lighting effects. Night scenes would be indicated by dress, dialogue, and perhaps burning torches.**

Work out **two different ways** of staging the sleepwalking scene on the Shakespearean stage. The two ways should give a different emphasis to the scene. You will need to think about such points as the following:

- entrances and exits;
- relation of the actors to the audience (do you want them to be near or far away? do the actors play *to* the audience or not?);
- relation of the three actors to each other;
- moves – when and where do the actors move, and why?;
- styles of acting – natural (lifelike)? stylised? the same for all three characters?

Choose a sequence of 20–25 lines and decide how the actors should present them. Concentrate in particular on whom they are talking to, and the tone(s) of voice in which they speak.

Decide on how you are going to present your ideas to the class. For instance: you might prepare some large diagrams, you might walk through your versions of the scene or even act them out if you have time (and the nerve). . . . Or you could just tell them.

---

## STORIES

Work on the stories of Shakespeare's plays can be done initially without any reference to the stage – or even, at first, to their being stories that Shakespeare dramatised. There is a wide variety of stories and story types to be found in the plays, as only a brief random selection can make clear:

- a king who bargains power for love;
- children who defy their parents in order to marry;
- an isolated girl who gains by a trick a husband who despises her;
- a man hired to kill a child;
- a girl born in storm at sea;
- a man sworn to vengeance by a ghost;
- a despised monster who sees a drunkard as a god;
- an older black man married to a younger white woman.

Any of these or the many others available could serve as the kernel for a wide variety of work. What is the potential of this story? In what ways might this story be told? What seem to be the values implicit in the story? What does the story remind you of? Can we find similar stories in contemporary fiction/the media? Why do people tell this kind of story? The focus may not be on Shakespeare at all, but pupils will have encountered stories that they may recognise in the plays later.

To introduce and begin an investigation of the range of stories, each pupil can be given a card bearing a name and a sentence (e.g. 'PERDITA When I was a baby I was abandoned on a sea-coast by order of my father'). Mingling and reading each other's cards, they find the other characters that belong to their story. Groups could then investigate the possibilities of their story (analysing it, testing its potential, re-presenting it) before discussing the various types of story, if the initial selection had been made in order to demonstrate variety, or look at a group of similar stories, if the selection has been made to explore variety within similarity.

Teachers may judge that pupils need a grasp of the storyline, or some knowledge of it, before encountering the text of any particular play. How this is done will vary with purpose.

- Most direct is a simple read-through of a prepared summary. This will stick better in pupils' minds if the classroom is marked out to represent locations in the play and individual pupils with name cards stand for characters. For instance, for *A Midsummer Night's Dream* the classroom can be set up to establish two fundamental locations, the COURT OF ATHENS and the WOOD. It may be useful to go further, and establish the usual inhabitants of each area before embarking on the narrative (perhaps as a first move to establishing 'expert groups' who are going to do work on behalf of the rest of the class on various aspects of character and plot).
- Give a selection of plot elements and ask groups to re-present them as playlets. For instance, divide the class into four groups, each given a work card with some of the plot elements of one of the story strands from *A Midsummer Night's Dream* (the lovers, the fairies, the workmen, Pyramus and Thisbe), a selection of lines from the play, and the instruction 'Use the following information to make up a play with at

least three scenes. Aim for a happy ending. You must use three of the lines in your presentation.' The pupils may produce plot lines that differ in some details from those in the plays, but this need not matter; they will have been thinking narratively and dramatically, preparing themselves not only for what they will find in Shakespeare but for thinking about what they will find.

Some teachers, perhaps finding the stories ideologically suspect, will want to question them sharply. A current method for doing this is 'changing stories' – conscious rewritings in alternative forms. As this can too easily be an inert remaking according to our own clichés, a method which allows pupils to experience some of the tensions between the stories and our preferences and expectations may be preferable. As, for instance, in this approach to *A Winter's Tale* (devised for Year 11 pupils, but adaptable for younger classes):

> Pupils work in trios to prepare the first stage. Each trio is made up of a character (Hermione, Polixenes, Camillo, or Antigonus) with a card outlining a dilemma, and two advisers, one positive and one negative. The advisers' task is to prepare the character for his or her part in a sequence of improvised scenes. The advisers can only advise – the choice of action is left to the character. Pupils can ask for additional background information and clarification of the task, but not for further information about the plot. After preparation, the pupils work through a series of improvisations based on scenes from the play, in which the teacher role-plays Leontes. Although no text is used, the tensions of the plot are beginning to be explored, and modern preferences will certainly figure in the pull between current assumptions about sexual morality and the absolute belief in marriage that the plot demands.

As in this example, the introduction to the plot might be deliberately partial. Pupils can then be introduced to how Shakespeare worked it out.

Approaches like those outlined above have advantages over the use of already written prose versions, even of the quality of Leon Garfield's *Shakespeare Stories*, although the latter also have their possibilities. For some classes narrative versions like Garfield's might come *after* a study of the play. Similarly video versions might come best after introductory work: pupils watch with expectations and questions, whether explicitly framed or not, having done their own work with some of the materials involved. However, the element of time may lead some teachers to feel that reading a good narrative version still makes the most economical introduction.

Also in the interests of getting the story established without getting 'bogged down in the language', teachers might begin with severely edited versions of the play. The Macmillan Dramascript abridgements offer such versions, but they have the disadvantage of foreclosing a good many questions by providing overdetailed stage directions that have no authorial status.

Given Shakespeare's skill in shaping a scene from narrative elements (finding dramatic potential in a story), work on plot elements can contain much that is not only worth while in its own right, not only useful as introductions to specific plays, but also genuinely exploratory of some of the central dramatic/thematic issues. However, given that the depth of Shakespeare's drama is enacted in his language, and that it is in the language that the most difficulty is found, there comes a stage in work with narrative when teachers have to consider whether or not it has passed over into evasion of what is arguably centrally Shakespearean.

## LANGUAGE

Whatever approaches we adopt to help our pupils come to terms with Shakespeare's language, we should bear in mind that Eliot's dictum 'All genuine poetry can communicate before it is understood' might be true. It is probable that Shakespeare's language grips at first in particular phrases or passages, sensed as somehow fine or mysterious, or as striking a chord with the individual's feelings or preoccupations (even if – as may well be the case – the words have been misunderstood). It might even be argued that, the story and dramatic situation being clearly established, we should to a large extent leave the language to take care of itself. However, we need to take seriously the panic that pupils feel at times with Shakespeare, that tells them that they don't understand anything when actually they understand quite a lot, and which inhibits them and curtails their interest.

It seems reasonable to suggest that there are four main sources, beyond the general air of antiquity and unfamiliarity, of the difficulties experienced by beginning readers of Shakespeare:

- **vocabulary** (any number of individual words they simply do not know, either because they no longer have currency or their currency is in some degree specialised);
- **allusion** (to, for instance, a range of classical mythology pupils may never have come across – should this factor enter into our choice of what myths and legends we tackle in early school?);
- **syntax** (especially in long sentences, since it's so easy to lose the 'spine' – fail to identify subject and main verb, especially when the difficulty is compounded by unusual vocabulary or highly wrought metaphor);
- **metaphor** (especially that which is intrinsic/organic, rather than illustrative or decorative, in relation to what is being said).

We need to be clear, as far as we can be, which types of difficulty (usually in combination) are likely to be experienced with particular passages, so that we can anticipate questions, make the helpful move without clutter, or make use of an appropriate exercise. The awareness needs to inform our preparation. The rest of this section indicates something of the range of approaches, beyond straight explication (which I am old-fashioned enough to believe still has a place), available to classroom teachers.

Several techniques have been developed for familiarising pupils with short passages – rarely longer than a speech – to enable them to get something of a feel for the language, to get it on their tongue, before comprehension has become an issue. A chief aim of some of these techniques is to give an equal responsibility to each member of the class for the text, so that none feel either unduly prominent or left out. Some examples:

- Each pupil has a scrap of text – no more than a brief sentence – on a card or piece of paper. They walk around the classroom repeating their lines – speaking, muttering, whispering, screaming; quickly, slowly . . . – until they are thoroughly familiar with them. They then use the lines to 'say' a variety of things to each other: using the line as a death threat, a loving greeting, a joke, etc. The lines must be carefully selected, with a clear sense of further possibilities to be explored (what kind of story might these lines come from? divide into 'nice' and 'nasty' groups according to feel of lines, etc.). This approach could be used as a prologue to one of the 'story' approaches; groups are given some of the lines the class have been playing with to use in their presentation.
- The class stand in a circle, the teacher in the centre. The teacher gives each pupil in turn a portion of the speech (no more than two lines at the most) to be worked on. The pupil repeats the line and tries to retain it while the others hear their lines. (This is the tricky bit, and sometimes it may be preferable for them to have the line, or the whole speech, on paper.) After a couple of practices round the circle, the speech can now be played with: shuffle the circle and speak the speech from the new positions; each pupil in turn 'takes the line a walk' across the circle to the pupil who speaks next (maintaining eye contact all the way); pupils mill about, avoiding contact, shouting the speech as their cues come; the same, running; one pupil stands, sits or kneels in the centre of the circle and has the speech spoken to him or her.
- To get the feel of blank verse: pupils have the text of a speech, which is group-spoken as they walk, five stresses per line, changing direction at the end of each line. After they have the hang of this they try with 'prosed' texts, working out the feel of when to turn.

In such approaches, the 'fun' element – the challenge of the game – effectively relegates or postpones questions of meaning while familiarising pupils with some of the language. Other exercises can foreground elements of meaning more specifically. For instance:

- Pupils stand in clusters of three to five, each with a copy of the speech being used. In turn, the groups read aloud together to the teacher up to a punctuation mark: the teacher quizzes them and they reply (shouting is encouraged in this exercise):

  *Pupils*: Is this a dagger that I see before me?
  *Teacher*: Is this a WHAT?
  *Pupils*: A DAGGER!
  *Teacher*: That you see WHERE?
  *Pupils*: BEFORE ME!!

  With careful selection this exercise can point to the relation between words in the passage, giving pupils a firmer grasp of the syntax and therefore the situation.
- Pupils can also be helped by being encouraged, in an appropriate passage, to point on the referring words or expressions at the person, place, thing – or even the concept – referred to. This can both clarify the meaning and display the feeling of lines most effectively: 'Thou, thou, Lysander, hast given her rhymes, / And interchang'd love-tokens with my child: / Thou hast by moonlight at her window sung . . .'
- Individuals are given slips, each containing a fragment of text, and informed that someone else has a fragment that goes with it. Their task is to go round reading each others' lines until they have paired up and can give the reasons for the pairing. The pairs of lines are then spoken out loud and what makes them pairs discussed. Pairs of lines of various kinds can be prepared: question and answer, echoed words and phrases; rhyme; syntactical parallels; metaphor. A few examples from *A Midsummer Night's Dream*:

(a)  The more I hate, the more he follows me.
        The more I love, the more he hateth me.
(b)              You perhaps may think
     Because she is something lower than myself
     That I can match her.
              Lower? Hark, again!
(c)  Your hands than mine are quicker for a fray
        My legs are longer, though, to run away!
(d)  I would my father look'd but with my eyes.
        Rather your eyes must with his judgement look.

- If a class have read a play up to a particular point, they could be given a prose summary of the next section together with a selection of lines that they are to relate to the action, saying who they think speaks them, to whom, in what circumstances. As with the similar use of lines in presenting plot elements, described above, the aim here may not be so much to be right as to explore possibilities.

Using these techniques will not get a class through a whole play, of course. There remains a necessary place for sustained reading; it is hard to see how a whole play can be got through in class without it. In some extended reading, the technique of reading around the class from punctuation mark to punctuation mark can still be used, but it is only one technique among many, and it can reduce the effect of the drama in some passages (it is better suited to sustained passages such as soliloquies). In passages of obvious confrontation or intense interaction between two characters it can be effective to divide the class into two, each rehearsing one set of lines before coming together. There are advantages if the half-class follow a lead voice – as long as the reader is receptive to ideas about variation of tone and pace. An undifferentiated roar is to be avoided.

But as well as the whole-class approach, we should not neglect the skilful deployment of our more fluent and/or (they are not always the same) dramatically competent readers. If we ourselves read Shakespeare well, we should not overlook ourselves as resources. A good reading can illuminate syntactic relations and dramatic qualities more suddenly than any amount of explanation.

We should also give opportunities for prepared readings, and for the less fluent to struggle with the text, if they wish to do so. In preparing pupils to attempt a comparatively unaided reading of Shakespeare there are a number of useful tips we can give them in addition to what they may have picked up tacitly from exercises of the kind described above. We can tell them that like us the Elizabethans contracted words, but differently (i', 'tis); that 'ere' is pronounced 'air' and means 'before'; that 'fie' rhymes with 'high' and is an expression of disgust or disapproval; that inversion of word order is fairly common etc. Some pupils genuinely appear to find 'thou' and its variants difficult (although this may be one word that they latch on to as identifiable among a general strangeness), so a bit of practice using it may help, getting the agreements right (thou hast, etc.). And so on.

Some help will be afforded by notes in the editions used. Pupils (and teachers) do find it comfortable to refer to them, and they are often genuinely useful. However, the tendency of most modern school editions (the honourable exception is the *Cambridge School Shakespeare*[3]) is to overexplain, or not to explain when explanation is really needed. Opinion will vary about this, but there is a lot to be said for plain text, texts with minimal notes, and texts with notes at the back.

During or after (or even, in some cases, before) class reading the text, there are a number of approaches to chosen sections of the text that can assist with comprehension. These include:

- Sequencing

    Choose a speech. Cut it up in two different ways, producing two sets of eight slips of card, each with a few lines on it. Working in pairs, some pupils attempt to sequence one version, some the other, and then compare notes. Groups could prepare sequencing exercises for each other. The cuts should be made in places where there are sufficient clues.

- Chaining

    Pupils annotate excerpts of text, indicating all the elements that give the passage cohesion, such as: sound patterns; grammar; related ideas; metaphors/images/ideas; rhetorical patterns. Instructions can indicate explicitly the types of connection to look for.

- Matching

    A sequence of text is given with some modern equivalents of some of the words/expressions in it printed at the bottom; pupils find the words in the speech. This can be developed into a study of the syntax of units of information. More rapidly, something of this can be done orally: 'Find me the bit that means . . .' can provide quick and accurate identifications, not always from the most able pupils.

- Editing

    Pupils study a passage and decide which words and phrases are in need of marginal explanation (it might be an idea to limit them to, say, two every fifty lines), and then attempt to supply them. They could then compare the glosses given in various editions. For more advanced editing work, pupils can be given Folio and Quarto parallel texts and invited to produce an edited and modernised version from them. Also they could work on acting editions. What can be cut without loss? (Very little, they might decide.) Can any artful substitutions of modern words be made? (Should they be?)

- Drawing

    Pupils can be invited to produce illustrations representing particular moments in the play. These might illustrate local metaphors ('Your eyes are lode-stars, and your tongue's sweet air/More tunable than lark to shepherd's ear') or explore response to a highly resonant moment (Hermia's dream: 'Methought a serpent ate my heart away/And you sat smiling at his cruel prey.').

When to bring in any of the exercises outlined in this section is a matter of judgement and tact in particular teaching situations. A sense of what is appropriate for this class/pupil on this occasion is essential, as also is a clear idea of where we might be going later. How much explanation, to whom, when? To what extent should we correct pupils' instinctive or even considered meaning-making when it goes awry? We can only feel our way and build up our experience.

## TOWARDS A PROGRAMME FOR KS3 AND KS4

In the foregoing no consistent attempt has been made to allocate any of the methods to specific years, because all are capable of development at a variety of levels. In this last section, however, a brief outline is offered of what a Shakespeare programme over five years might look like.

### Key Stage 3

In **Year 7**, a 'sampling' approach can be used to give pupils the idea of Shakespeare as rich and varied, well worth exploring, and to be looked forward to, as well as introducing them to some of the working methods that will be used during the key stage. A number of units can either be taught in one sequence as a Shakespeare induction course or be spaced out over a longer period. Such a programme might include:

- work on playscript (as part of a programme on varieties of writing);
- some playing with storylines (perhaps in relation to a unit on narrative, perhaps involving appropriate myths and legends);
- design and presentation of playlets on some of the main plots of a particular play;
- particular problems of dramatic representation: for instance, (i) pupils are given a list of the players, the basic facts of the Hamlet–Laertes duel and some of the lines from the scene, the task being to produce a set of five tableaux, each with a spoken line, to tell a version of the story; (ii) pupils are told about the director's problem of whether or not to bring Banquo's ghost on stage, and invited to try it out both ways (without text);
- production work on a short and accessible scene with text (*Macbeth* Act 1 Scene 1 is an obvious example);
- 'Design a Fairy'; worksheet with names of fairies from *A Midsummer Night's Dream*, some key speeches, and the instruction to design a fairy in terms of appearance, clothing, style of speech, way of moving, etc., with quotations from the text related to design – or a similar exercise on Ariel and Caliban;
- a presentation, by whatever means – description, reading, prepared

acting (perhaps with help from an older class) – of a scene that the teacher particularly likes (it is important that the children become aware that we are ourselves interested in Shakespeare);
* an introduction to Shakespeare's playhouse;
* an 'Introducing Shakespeare' booklet, containing a range of information (life, plots, playhouse, some characters, miscellaneous items of information) and activities (involving research in the library);
* watching a play, perhaps an adaptation (preferably in 'theatrical space' rather than on video);
* display work/celebration.

In **Year 8** (during which some of the above approaches could also be used), some short extracts from Shakespeare (for instance, the winter song from *Love's Labour's Lost*) could be introduced in poetry work, perhaps with a KAL bias (if the poems are presented in their 'original' spelling and punctuation). Some of the elements touched on in Year 7 can be revisited and expanded, and new work introduced along the following lines:

* theatrical devices such as soliloquy and aside;
* questions of staging, perhaps in relation to particular scenes;
* an investigation of a theme or narrative element and some instances of it in Shakespeare: e.g. death, murder, haunting, persuasion, madness, love at first sight, fathers and daughters (the emphasis can usefully be on dramatic realisation/stagecraft, a variety of techniques being used to explore and present the scenes).

In these approaches more text can be introduced than in Year 7, perhaps in the form of edited leaflets. As this work can be much more demanding, it might be best delayed until the Summer term.

In **Year 9** the Shakespeare work will be concentrated mainly on a full text using a combination of the approaches discussed above. It is to be hoped that by this stage the pupils have some interest in Shakespeare, some familiarity with elements of the plays and some of the classroom activities. They will not be coming to any texts cold – a fact which should go some way to relieving anxiety all round.

### Key Stage 4

Curiously, KS4 has been to date less demanding than KS3 had become, with no requirement to study a complete play or to sit examination questions on Shakespeare. The 1995 Order, however, does require the reading of two complete plays at KS3 and 4. As yet we do not know what the examination requirements will be, but we may hope that there will still be opportunity for coursework approaches, and it is on these that we should continue to concentrate. To a large extent we may be able to continue with previous approaches that have proved successful. They can also be used with texts studied for an examination, but would need to be supplemented with revision exercises and exam practice based on careful analysis of the kinds of question set by the particular board.

In addition to essays of the more traditional type, coursework might include any of the following:

- A development of the thematic approach touched on in KS3: comparison, for instance, of first meetings of men and women (Romeo and Juliet, Petruchio and Katherine); hauntings; murder (perhaps comparing *Macbeth* Act 2 Scene 2 with the murder scene in *Woodstock*, which *may* be by Shakespeare – there is no reason we should not go to the fringes of or outside the canon).
- Production-based work. Groups might work on

  - a set, lighting;
  - casting and costuming;
  - a scene that is controversial in interpretation (the end of *Measure for Measure*, for instance);
  - moments of tricky but important transition from scene to scene (e.g. the first and second scenes of *The Tempest*);
  - different ways of staging and playing soliloquies.

  Groups should compare notes, seeing how their ideas modify one another. Groups working on particular scenes could produce a detailed prompt-copy.

  Pupils might also write reviews of contrasting productions on stage or screen, with particular attention to key scenes or features.
- After studying a play, a group could look at some abridgements and retellings for younger readers, considering how successful the authors have been. A comparison of Leon Garfield and Mary Lamb on one play – including the assumptions that they make about their audiences – could be a fruitful piece of coursework. Pupils might also undertake their own retellings for younger classes.
- A study of the idea of a classic literature. What are the classic literatures of different cultures? Does any culture not have a classic literature? Do classic literatures have anything in common? How does Shakespeare – how do other classic literatures – permeate society? Which stories or story-types are transcultural? Why? Which, if any, are not?

Pupils who have followed a programme such as this will have been given opportunities to experience and explore Shakespeare that may lead to insights into a heritage more interesting and challenging than the monolithic and unexamined 'good thing' envisaged in some notions of National Curriculum Shakespeare.

## ACKNOWLEDGEMENTS

This chapter is much indebted to the work of the Shakespeare and Schools project (in particular to sessions led by Rex Gibson and John Salway) and to the work of colleagues in Derbyshire (particularly Bob Cunningham).

## REFERENCES AND FURTHER READING

1.  DES (1989) *English for Ages 5 to 16*, HMSO
2.  *Shakespeare and Schools* (Three issues a year for £5 from Rex Gibson at Cambridge Institute of Education, Shaftesbury Road, Cambridge CB2 2BX)
3.  *Cambridge School Shakespeare* (1991–) Cambridge University Press

Boagey, Eric (1988) *Starting Shakespeare*, Unwin Hyman, London
DES (1990) *English in the National Curriculum*, HMSO
Gibbs, Gerard (1991) 'Shakespeare on film and the National Curriculum', *The Use of English*, Spring
Gibson, Rex (1990) *Secondary School Shakespeare*, Cambridge Institute of Education
Haddon, John (1993) '"I Was Macbeth's Kilt-Maker" Or, What are we making of Shakespeare?', *The Use of English*, Spring
Leach, Susan (1992) *Shakespeare in the Classroom*, Open University Press, Milton Keynes
Leach, Susan *Shakespeare in the Classroom* (A practical pack on classroom activities, available from the author at 17 Glenelg Mews, Beacon Road, Walsall, West Midlands, WS5 3LG)
NCC (1993) National Curriculum Council Consultative Report: English in the National Curriculum, NCC, York
O'Brien, Veronica (1982) *Teaching Shakespeare*, Edward Arnold, London
Reynolds, Peter (1991) *Practical Approaches to Teaching Shakespeare*, Oxford University Press
SCAA (1994) *English in the National Curriculum: Draft Proposals (May 1994)*, Schools Curriculum & Assessment Authority
Sullivan, Theresa (1992) *Getting Into Shakespeare*, Longman, Harlow

# Chapter 9

# What use are the new technologies?

*Chris Abbott*

## INTRODUCTION

It is likely that almost everyone who has contributed to this book has done so with the help of a computer. Computers have changed our lives even more radically than machines changed the lives of the factory workers of a previous era. Just as our forebears lived through an industrial revolution, so we are moving through an information revolution in the later years of this century. To date, information technology has had only a gradual effect on our lives, an evolutionary rate of change rather than revolutionary transformation; but the changes are increasing by the day.

It is for this reason, amongst others, that the National Curriculum places the Information Technology Attainment Target within one subject, Technology, but requires it to be delivered across the whole curriculum. The Programmes of Study for IT capability are divided into two themes:

1  Communicating and handling information.
2  Using IT to investigate.

There is much here that speaks directly to the teacher of English, and which points to more of a role for IT than can be satisfied by the occasional use of a word processor. IT, like English, is about communication and information. As the Cox Committee stated in its interim document in 1988, 'most interactions with computers are language experiences. . . . This huge and expanding technology is therefore of great importance to teachers of English. And Information Technology should be seen as a way of encouraging pupils' language development'. Unfortunately, that comment did not survive into the National Curriculum English folder, and IT completely disappeared from the 1994 rewrite (SCAA, 1994). This was explained as being linked to the need to remove ambiguity, since cross-curricular IT was already required, but many commentators were unconvinced by this excuse and saw this removal as significant when viewed alongside what happened at the same time to Drama and Media Studies. (See chapter 10.)

## WRITING AND IT

Writers are being profoundly affected by IT, and it is vital that English lessons reflect this; the central place secured by IT capability in the National Curriculum makes this even more necessary. Computers appear in numerous aspects of our everyday life, increasingly in hidden form and often inside other equipment. The Windows interface which started life on computers is now appearing on photocopiers, fax machines and all kinds of other equipment.

Media Education needs to deal with this issue, and with the complex area of computer games. English teachers have always had an interest in the cultural artefacts that feature in their pupils' lives, and where once comics and television were studied in the classroom, it will become increasingly appropriate to look at the latest computer games or developments in electronic fiction. Just as one reason for investigating television in the classroom was to help young people view critically, so an attempt to bring computer culture into the study arena will help to meet some of the criticisms made of what is perceived to be the passive user of the technology.

It would be true to say that word processing is still the most frequent use to which a computer is put in English lessons. Word processors have totally changed the way that many people write, and for some young people they are the natural starting point for expressing thoughts in visible though changeable form. It is the malleability of word processing that is its strength, not its ability to print texts in a variety of different styles, colours and formats.

Only occasional users of the technology ourselves, teachers were slow to see that the ability to control printing is peripheral to the liberating effect the computer can have on the drafting process. Many of us in the early 1980s were delighted to see that a word processor enabled a child to correct misspelled words, change the construction of a sentence, add a whole new section and delete that which was repetitive, and still end up with a perfect printout rather than a handwritten page covered in corrections. Within a year or two, we were expecting that our perfect printout should be in 24pt Old English, or in green on a red background: many of us were seduced by what the technology could do, rather than by how it could help us express our thoughts.

It is true, nevertheless, that information technology has almost completely merged the twin technologies of writing and printing, separated for centuries until the arrival of the computer. A writer who has now become used to word processing would find it hard to believe that people ever produced lengthy revised documents in any other way. Writing a departmental policy used to be a matter of attempting to gain control of the pen or the minute book, since it was inevitable that ownership of

textual ideas always resided more with the wielder of the writing implement than with the other authors. With a word processing program, on
the other hand, there is no overt ownership; the text looks the same
whoever typed the words on the keyboard. Word processing, then, reduces
what Susan Zvacek calls 'the solitary nature of the writing process, facili-
tating the display of partially completed manuscripts for conferencing
and group editing' (Zvacek, 1992). If she had attended many staff
meetings, she might also have added that such an activity guards against
the danger of one writer attempting to speak for all.

The essential factor in all this is that the writing process changes when
a computer is the tool. As Colette Daiute told us several years ago, 'with
the computer as the instrument, writing is more like talking' (Daiute,
1985). Noel Williams has investigated this idea and looked at what he
calls 'talky writing,' and how it tends to be 'rightward-branching . . . the
thought emerges during the process of typing' (Holt and Williams, 1992).
Many research projects have tried to look at the nature of this change:
several, like the scheme in Hertfordshire involving every pupil in a year
group being given a notebook portable computer, not only showed
greatly increased motivation but a greater volume of writing. *Children do
not just write more with computers, they write differently.* In Hertfordshire the
teachers were very aware of the need for this use of computers to be
grounded in a sound understanding of the writing process. They concluded
that 'appropriate use of computer technology can transform language
development given a rational and informed approach to the process of
writing' (Breese, 1993).

Where so many of us misunderstood word processors when they first
appeared in our classrooms was in seeing them as devices which related
to what had gone before, such as the typewriter and the printing press.
Word processing is not copy typing followed by printing, but a revising
and drafting activity. As has been pointed out many times, 'when a writer
conducts a revision, he takes actions: addition, deletion, substitution and
rearrangement. . . . These actions are realised on a word processor by the
commands insert, delete, substitute and cut and paste' (Holt and
Williams, 1992). Some writers have gone so far as to suggest that use of a
word processor alters the thinking processes involved with writing, so
that the person involved thinks in blocks of meaning rather than in
individual words or ideas. A good example of this would be the writing
of a poem, perhaps beginning with a stream of consciousness approach.

One way of doing this is to switch off the monitors and ask pupils to
type on the keyboards and not be concerned by whether words are
misspelled or misplaced. When the monitors are switched back on the
blocks of meaning can be separated, repeated, deleted or moved as
necessary. Pupils will be helped to concentrate on meaning and effect
rather than surface issues such as spelling and punctuation, which can be

added more sensibly at the final stages, as would be done by many poets. In this activity, the computer plays the role of a tool which helps pupils work in a poet-like way; and the appearance of the words on the screen rather than on paper helps to draw attention to them and to focus the attention of the writer.

Many developers of software aiming to assist in planning before writing, or for the checking of spelling, grammar or style, see the writing process as being one that involves three clear stages. One of the biggest flaws in this very linear view of writing is the assumption that the process can be neatly divided into preparation for writing, the writing of a first draft, and then the revision of that draft. In fact, writing is both recursive and incapable of neat analogy, inextricably linked as it is to thought and emotion.

In the example given above of the use of a word processor to move from stream of consciousness to a finished poem, that movement is not in only one direction. It will sometimes be necessary to switch off the monitor again and seek more thoughts. One finished line may then seem inappropriate and will need radical rethinking or even deletion. Word processors encourage this recursive approach to writing by making it easy to do, and by removing the drudgery associated with revision using earlier tools such as pens and typewriters.

Spell-, grammar- and style-checking tools are aimed at what many see as the final stage of writing, where a rough draft is formed more fully, checked and refined. They may also have a role at a much earlier stage. Many spell-checkers include a thesaurus facility, a fascinating tool when at the service of a writer rather than controlling that person's writing. Synonyms can be looked up as in a book, but they can also be placed in the text to be seen in context, and a number of possibilities can be tried in rotation. Since every synonym leads to a changing list of other words, fascinating trails of meaning can be set up that take a writer down new paths of understanding. The writing of poetry, in particular, can be informed by judicious use of such a tool, so long as the poet and not the computer program is making the choices.

Outlining software is the name often given to a utility little used in education but one which offers much that is of interest. The essential idea is that the writer creates a plan in some form on the screen which can then be expanded and contracted as different areas of writing are undertaken. This is usually done by pointing and clicking at a section, so that it is very quick and easy to move around the text without losing track of the overall plan. Such tools could form a useful addition to the facilities available in a classroom and could reside on notebook computers which could be made available to groups or individuals for planning.

The ability of outliners to attach text to ideas makes them an interesting way of writing, and can lead to some fascinating work. One approach is to use the names of three protagonists as the first level of outlining. At lower levels can be attached their thoughts and feelings, and links can then be added to show the way they feel about each other. Expanding the outline will begin the process of writing a dialogue between these characters, and pupils will not be tempted to forget the essential differences between their characters as these are always present at different levels of the outline.

The addition of a modem and a telephone line enables a computer to communicate with any other computer which is similarly equipped, wherever that machine and its users might be. With the easy availability of electronic mail systems within education, writers can exchange text across counties, countries or continents, provided the language is a common one; and in time even this restriction will become much less important. For many years now, children in some schools have routinely exchanged writing with another establishment which none of them may ever have visited or even seen.

The even greater use of such technology in the USA means that many of the links have been with that country, but most of the developed world is now accessible. Events surrounding the fall of the Berlin Wall, to give one example, were of much greater significance to the south London school which was in daily electronic correspondence with young people in what had been the East German section of the city. Similarly, many British schools on the Campus system received a heart-rending message a while ago from a teacher hiding in a cellar during the siege of Vukovar in the former Yugoslavia. These texts were real, direct and highly motivating, as is any correspondence which puts young people in touch with their counterparts in other countries. The true horror of the fighting in Bosnia was brought home for many young people when they received answers to their questions about favourite television programmes and other leisure activities and discovered that these young people from a distant century liked the same trainers, the same music and watched the same episodes of Australian soap operas.

One of the biggest disappointments of electronic mail is that the various systems assume that everyone speaks English, or at least a language that uses the Roman alphabet. This means that for many young pupils in our schools there has been no possibility of communicating electronically in their own first language. The arrival of the fax machine has changed this, as has the availability of multilingual software such as Allwrite 2 which allows pupils to write in a wide range of languages with differing character sets and whether they are written left to right or right to left. Many more languages now carry equal status with English in the classroom in that they can be written and revised using a word processor.

## READING AND IT

For many years one of the most popular pieces of software on all kinds of educational computers has been Developing Tray, developed by Bob Moy and ILECC in London in the early 1980s. Often misrepresented, Developing Tray, used well, can convert a Luddite English teacher to the use of computers in a single session. Unimaginatively used, it can confirm that teacher's worst suspicions of computers as highly expensive ways of doing what was not educationally viable in the beginning. Essentially a mechanism for predicting texts, Developing Tray allows students to use all the powerful reading strategies they possess in order to read what they cannot see: a text in which all or most of the letters are missing. The crucial factor in the process is the choice of text; if the context and subject matter are relevant to the group, then the most surprising abilities can be unleashed.

One special school's unmotivated GCSE English group spent forty-five minutes predicting Wilfred Owen's 'Anthem for Doomed Youth'; if presented with the poem in an anthology they would have felt they had fully investigated the poem's potential after five minutes. They insisted on continuing into the break period and managed to reconstruct the whole text apart from the word 'orison', although they knew the required word was related to sound. Their scratchpad notes, kept as they made progress using the inbuilt facility of the program, showed their early awareness of the tone of the poem long before they had begun to uncover its incidental detail. The same group later took great delight in reconstructing every word of the first section of the head teacher's morning assembly, as tape-recorded and then transcribed into Developing Tray by their teacher. This led to a lively discussion of varieties of talk and the way in which we use repetition and control devices in speech.

News simulations are programs that involve pupils in reading and writing. They form one of the few computer activities which is possible where a class of thirty has access to only one computer. That computer plays the role of a telex machine, and the software package causes it to print news messages at predefined intervals, just as though it was doing so in a newsroom as a real event unfolded. Pupils can then be given a task to complete based on their reading of these messages. One such task involves reaction to Press Association telexes regarding the Hyde Park bombing. Pupils play the role of radio news bulletin writers, their task being to condense the information they receive, select what is most important, and write it in a style most appropriate for their role. An alternative would be for each group to be preparing the front page of a newspaper, possibly a very specific newspaper with an agenda of its own. In this case, it would obviously be preferable for each group to have its own computer with desktop publishing software in order to produce this newspaper page. Many sets of real messages are available for these programs, usually originating from one of the major news wire services. Teachers can also write their own, which gives great opportunity for the creation of activities which are relevant to the class or the work they are involved with at that time.

One particularly successful activity created by a teacher in this way involved a series of messages about the search for Lennie after he has killed Candy's wife in *Of Mice and Men*. The messages gave pupils extra information which they could include in the front page of the Californian newspaper they were asked to design. The aim of the activity was to encourage pupils to think about the historical context of the novel and the implications of Lennie's actions. The extra information they included in their newspapers also indicated their understanding of other issues raised in the book, such as the position of black workers like Crooks and the subservient role of women in the life of the ranch. Some pupils cleverly used other information gained from their reading, such as the liking of some ranch-hands for writing to magazines and newspapers, and there were many advertisements for workers such as Lennie and George.

All kinds of text are now available in electronic form, especially on CD-ROM. To begin with, the emphasis was on works which are out of copyright, but this is changing and we are beginning to see writers exploring the potential of the medium. The first CD-ROMs tended to be books transferred to the new medium; they had extra features, especially in relation to surface stylistic searches of text, but they did not attempt to explore the interactive possibilities as more recent resources have done. It is likely that leisure or entertainment areas will lead the way here, with feature films already being made with alternative sections which do not appear at the cinema but could form alternative routes for the CD-ROM version. In particular, the vast potential for storing lengthy texts cheaply in electronic form makes it likely that less wealthy readers will in future be able to own much greater quantities of texts, if they choose to do so. On the other hand, if electronic communications systems continue to grow, there will be no need to own any texts, since whatever is desired can be requested through a modem and delivered to a personal computer instantly: the viewer of a television arts programme interested in the review of a book could instantly switch to text retrieval, call up the book and read it at their leisure, the cost being added to their monthly information systems bill. Such technology already exists and is available in some parts of the world for specific titles.

Reading from a computer screen is very different from reading from a paper-based medium. The text is usually in a different plane, it glows from within and can often be customised to meet the preferences of a particular reader. If anything, the process would seem more like reading

a medieval parchment roll than a printed book, with the text appearing to scroll up and down past the computer screen. Much work remains to be done on the optimum amount of text to be placed on a screen, and the size of text likely to be appropriate for the average user, although these are issues being explored by many researchers already.

## TALKING AND LISTENING

The National Oracy Project uncovered many examples of effective talk motivated by computers, some of it documented with the help of NCET. 'The computer', they found, 'is an effective catalyst of talk both at the screen and away from it. . . . Of particular interest is the talk which takes place at the computer screen, for it can differ significantly from small group talk in other contexts' (Kemeny, 1990). IT has been undervalued here, but it is a great motivator and channeller of discussion and discourse. The use of Developing Tray to reconstruct a poem often provokes talk of a structured and thoughtful nature which is not oppositional. Pupils attempting to rebuild a poem on the computer screen are sitting side by side and united in a common task. As computers begin to talk there are other possibilities – and, rather further ahead, lies the opportunity of the listening computer, as speech recognition is refined and developed.

Many of the earliest uses of computers in English lessons revolved around the reading of adventures, or adventure games as they became unfairly known. Not unrelated to the Dungeons and Dragons interactive storybooks also popular in the early 1980s, these were often sexist, occasionally racist and mostly dull. Improvements occurred, however, and by the mid 1980s the more exciting possibilities of adventure authoring programs began to emerge. One program used by many schools was Hazard and Rescue, a traditionally structured authoring system based on the quest genre. One class spent many hours devising an adventure based in their own school and relating to the problems of being bullied. Strategies for dealing with bullies were discussed and included in the game, the processes of bullying were analysed and attention was paid to whether the design of buildings can be a contributory factor. All of these issues were included in the adventure written and later played by the group.

The decisions needed to devise such an adventure formed an excellent group task, leading to complex discussions of genre, register and meaning. Many useful resources were developed by teachers, and a number of publishers produced simulations of real-life dilemmas such as hunger in the developing world or the decisions facing a person considering activities carrying a high HIV risk. The use of news simulations as already described also carries great potential for focused discussion and structured debate.

With the late 1980s came the rise of the computer game, a medium characterised not just by silent concentration, the phenomenon most recognised by parents, but by active and complex discourse with other players, usually unobserved by parent or teacher. Rather like having seen the latest episode of *Neighbours*, knowledge of the latest computer game and a knowledge of its idiosyncrasies can be the way in which a young person socialises and establishes contact with new acquaintances of the same age. The study of computer games as media offers fertile ground for the future and it is likely to refer back to many of the activities now taken for granted in the study of television and film.

Standard English is an issue as computers become more talkative, and it is certainly true that many computers speak a mainly male and American English, the correctness of which is governed by far different rules from those assumed by politicians. The addition of a speech syn-thesiser or digitised speech to a computer enables it to speak in a wide variety of ways. Disabled users of speech output devices attached to computers sometimes select different voices for different purposes, per-haps using a stern voice when talking to the bank manager or a more relaxed conversational tone when talking on the telephone. It is inter-esting to note that the first sign of governmental interest in speech and computers came when a minor study of reading age gain attempted to prove rapid and large improvements in reading attainment following the use of a talking word processor. This was followed by a surge in sales of the software used in the project, but not by any sign of DfE sponsorship to acquire more equipment capable of speech.

## MANAGEMENT ISSUES

1  Computers must be readily available and not need setting up as if they were of use for special occasions only. They are tools like pens and paper, and should therefore be provided for pupils until the not-too-distant day when almost all children in the class will have their own.

2  One computer in a classroom, or even two or three, is unlikely to be a truly appropriate resource. On the other hand, it is almost certainly not necessary for every child to have one, and collaborative writing is one of the most effective ways of using a computer. Any doubters regarding this need only engage in such an exercise with their colleagues.

3  There are even greater management issues related to reading and IT than to writing. The issue is not just how many computers, but how powerful they should be, which electronic information systems they should be connected to, and what resources should be bought for them.

4  For many schools this is all in the future, although the government

supplied every secondary school with one CD-ROM system as long ago as 1992. Unfortunately, no software was supplied with it and little that was suitable was available at the time. It is vital that the English department is represented on the school subcommittee that decides on the purchase of such resources, since each CD-ROM can cost a great deal of money. There are cheaper resources but in many cases they are of dubious value, such as the CD-ROM of the collected Sherlock Holmes stories which was purchased by many schools but used by few.

5  The CD-ROM version of the *Oxford English Dictionary*, on the other hand, is a fascinating and valuable resource. Although it costs several hundred pounds, it does enable users to search by definition as well as by word, or to look at word origin and search for particular influences, offering fertile ground for knowledge about language activities. Although it sounds expensive, it costs less than the twenty-volume book version of the same publication.

6  Where talk and computers are concerned there are difficult issues to be faced with regard to classroom practice. One aspect which is of crucial importance is where the computers are to be placed and how pupils will sit in relation to them. The traditional computer laboratory layout is totally unsuitable, since it involves computers in a U-shape with one or two users in front of each machine. Far more useful is a group-based plan with computers on island tables around the room. The monitors should be on tilt and swivel stands for health and safety reasons, but this also enables different groups of pupils to use the same computer. It is this which should be borne in mind when choosing a computer, as another essential component is a separate keyboard with a lead long enough to reach anyone around the table.

7  These management issues are complex and need constant review. For many years we argued for access to the computer room for English teachers in secondary schools, or for the school computer in a primary school to be used for word processing as well as maths activities. Now that those battles have been largely won or are no longer appropriate we have a general acceptance of the computer as a cross-curricular multimedia tool; but where should it be based, and how should it be made available? For many schools, the library forms at least part of the answer, especially with regard to access to electronic information systems. If a CD-ROM encyclopaedia is roughly analogous to a set of books, then surely it should reside alongside those books. The situation becomes less clear when we look at interactive fiction on CD-ROM, which has more in common with the lending section of the library, or the classroom book-box.

8  The library is probably not the place to read electronic fictional texts; they rightly belong to the classroom, the bus going home, the child's bedroom or some other private and comfortable environment. Whether

access will be available in such areas depends on the speed with which the hardware, the equipment for viewing such texts, becomes smaller and cheaper. Most experts agree that it will happen, and in only a few years; the disagreement begins when one tries to be more precise about the time-scale. Our task now is to prepare young people for a future in which electronic books will be in every home and most writing will be done using some form of word processor, a situation which is likely to be reached in the early years of the next century.

## CONCLUSION

The tremendous advances being made in multimedia and picture-based systems mean that we are on the threshold of exciting change, as 'the electronic medium gives renewed prominence to the long discredited art of writing with pictures' (Bolter, 1991). Children in some schools already routinely fill the role of multimedia authors, writing with text, pictures, sound and moving images. Within a few years, virtual reality tools will enable them to create whole-story environments where once they could only write words. The important benefit will remain, however, the essential revisionary capabilities of information technology. What is important is not that a child can create a text with moving video inserts and spoken passages, but that all three can be changed as often as necessary, re-thought, improved and saved in that better version. It is the role of IT to help us communicate more effectively, more clearly, more quickly and to more people over greater distances; and it is likely to be the young people in our schools who do this effectively before those of us who have lived through the birth and early years of the technology even begin to do so.

## REFERENCES AND FURTHER READING

Abbott, C (1990) 'Learning with computers', *Language and Learning No. 2*, Questions Publishing Company

Abbott, C (1990) 'Word processing for special needs', *The British Journal of Special Education*, March

Abbott, C (1993) 'IT and English: looking ahead', *The English Magazine*, No. 28, The English and Media Centre

Abbott, C and Davidson, J (1990) 'What's in IT for English?', *The English Magazine*, No. 24, The English and Media Centre

Bolter, J D (1991) *Writing Space: The Computer, Hypertext and the History of Writing*, Lawrence Erlbaum Associates, NJ

Breese, C (1993) 'Computers and the writing process: a memo to the Head', in Monteith, M (ed) *Computers and Language*, Intellect, Oxford

Daiute, C (1985) *Writing and Computers*, Addison-Wesley

Hartley, J (ed) (1992) *Technology and Writing: Reading in the Psychology of Written Communication*, Jessica Kingsley Publishers

Holt, P and Williams, N (ed) (1992) *Computers and Writing: State of the Art*, Intellect, Oxford

Keith, G (1991) *Knowledge about Language*, NCET

Kemeny, H (ed) (1990) *Talking it Through*, report from the National Oracy Project, NCET

Lynch, W (1991) *Planning for Language*, NCET

Minns, H (1991) *Primary Language*, NCET

Monteith, M (1993) *Computers and Language*, Intellect, Oxford

Moore, P and Tweddle, S (1992) *The Integrated Classroom: Language, Learning and IT*, NCET

SCAA (1994) *English in the National Curriculum: Draft Proposals (May 1994)*, Schools Curriculum & Assessment Authority

Tweddle, S (ed) (1992) *Developing English: Approaches with IT*, NATE

Zvacek, S (1992) 'Word-processing and the teaching of writing', in Hartley, J (ed) *Technology and Writing: Reading in the Psychology of Written Communication*, Jessica Kingsley Publishers

# Chapter 10

# What is left of drama and media?

*Nick McGuinn*

## INTRODUCTION

Drama and media education[1] were both excluded from the charmed circle of National Curriculum 'core' and 'foundation' subjects established by the Education Reform Act of 1988. Despite official assurances that the foundation subjects were 'certainly *not* a complete curriculum',[2] the consequences of exclusion have proved serious: no nation-wide debate about subject content and purpose; no statutory orders based on a ten-level model of continuity and progression; no government-sponsored training programme; no compulsory assessment arrangements.

The members of the National Curriculum English Working Group acknowledged the long-established relationship between the three subject areas[3] and attempted to win both drama and media education some measure of official recognition[4] by making space for them in their report *English for Ages 5 to 16*. As the 1994 Draft Proposals (SCAA, 1994) for the revision of the 1990 Order threatened to alter radically the relationship between the three subjects, it is important to recall exactly why the members of the Cox Committee sought to preserve those links. They stressed the ways in which drama and media education could enrich the English curriculum:

> Drama can make an important contribution towards realising the overall aims of English set out in chapters 2 and 3 of this Report. For example, drama contributes to personal growth, by enabling pupils to express their emotions and by helping them to make sense of the world, and to preparation for adult life through such activities as the simulation of meetings.

> Pupils use drama to gain insights into moral and social issues in works of literature. They can also use the medium to explore character or linguistic or structural features of texts.

> We have considered media education largely as part of the exploration of contemporary culture, alongside more traditional literary texts.

Above all, drama and media education were valued for the fact that they could provide powerful and varied contexts for language use:

> Drama quickly reveals to children the effectiveness of language, building up their language resources and allowing them to develop an awareness of a whole range of linguistic choices and registers.

> Media education, like drama, deals with fundamental aspects of language, interpretation and meaning. It is therefore consonant with the aims of English teaching.

> (DES, 1989b)

The problem with the Cox Working Group's approach was that it relegated drama and media education to the status of service subjects which were acknowledged only in so far as they answered the requirements of the English Order. The 1994 Draft Proposals took this position to an extreme which had to be moderated in the 1995 Orders. The 1994 Programme of Study for Speaking and Listening at Key Stages 3 and 4 – to cite one example – said that pupils:

> should participate in a wide range of drama activities to develop their communication skills and their ability to evaluate language use.

> (SCAA, 1994)

Other major aspects of drama – its 'power to move and evoke' (Hornbrook, 1991); the complexities of stagecraft – are dismissed as unspecified 'elements' which pupils need to do no more than 'consider'. The 1995 version improves on this slightly in suggesting that students 'should be given opportunities to consider significant features of their own and others' performances'.

The same concern can be expressed about media education. The Programme of Study for Attainment Target 2 at Key Stages 3 and 4 says that pupils should:

> reflect upon the use of language in a variety of media, making comparisons where appropriate, e.g. . . . . *a comparison of a television news bulletin with a report on the same event in a newspaper.*

> (SCAA, 1994)

There is no requirement there for 'a wider consideration of how texts are produced and circulated, and of how they represent their subject matter' (Bowker, 1991). As a result of criticisms in the consultation period, the 1995 Programme added:

> Pupils should be introduced to a wide range of media, e.g. *magazines, newspapers, radio, television, film.* They should be given opportunities to analyse and evaluate such material, which should be of high quality

and represent a range of forms and purposes, and different structural and presentational devices.

(DFE, 1995)

Even so, this (with the accompanying 'consider how texts are changed when adapted to different media') goes little further than Cox's original proposals.

Since drama and media education are perceived as subordinate to English rather than valued as subjects in their own right, no serious attempt is made to plan for continuity or progression in either area. Under the heading of *Range* for Attainment Target 1 at Key Stage 1, the Orders state that pupils should be encouraged:

> to participate in drama activities, improvisation and performance of varying kinds, using language appropriate to a role or situation.

At Key Stage 2 (and in virtually the same words at stages 3 and 4):

> Pupils should be given opportunities to participate in a wide range of drama activities, including improvisation, role-play and the writing and performance of scripted drama.

(SCAA, 1994)

It is enough that the pupils should 'participate' or that they should 'experience a widening range of drama activities'. There is no question of teaching them to become more adept at story-telling, improvising or performing. No attempt is made to work out precisely what teachers might expect the average 7-year-old, for example, to know, understand or do in terms of dramatic skill; nor to consider how these skills should have been enhanced by the time that same child reached the age of 11 or 14.

Media education fares worse than this. The only reference in the first two Key Stages is the vague suggestion that pupils 'should be taught to identify and comment on key features of what they see and hear in a variety of media' (*Speaking and Listening*, KS2). This despite the fact that, in a publication which appeared more than a year before the 1990 English Order, the British Film Institute's Primary Working Party had argued that children should 'begin to follow a programme of study in media education' from the age of five (Bazalgette, 1989). Media texts do not figure at all in the level descriptions.

Why should English teachers be concerned about these inconsistencies? It is useful, again, to recall the Proposals of the English Working Group chaired by Professor Cox. The Working Group members made English teachers responsible for ensuring the survival of specialist courses in drama and media studies at Key Stage 4:

> By using drama as a part of the learning process, English teachers will be providing experiences for pupils which will help them make an

informed choice when considering drama as a subject option, whether for GCSE or as part of a non-examined course in combined or expressive arts.

And again:

The English curriculum should prepare pupils for possible study of these subjects [Media Education and IT] as separate options. . . .
(DES, 1989b)

What are these areas which English teachers must take into account if they are to help their pupils make 'informed choices' about specialist drama and media courses at Key Stage 4? The British Film Institute and the Arts Council have offered some suggestions. In 1989, the BFI published its 'proposed attainment targets for media education'. The proposals were offered as 'a basis for discussion' only and were limited, therefore, to 'two main levels of attainment, headed Level 3 and Level 5' (Bazalgette, 1989). Three years later the Arts Council, eager to 'add to [National Curriculum Council] documentation its view of drama as an art form with its own distinct discipline and methodology' (Arts Council, 1992), went further by publishing Programmes of Study and End of Key Stage Statements for pupils at 7, 11, 14 and 16.

These documents provide a significant gloss on the English Order. The BFI publication proposes six attainment targets based on six media areas: *agencies, categories, technologies, languages, audiences* and *representations*. The Arts Council's Programmes of Study are divided into three: *Making, Performing* and *Responding*.

The proposals share several important characteristics, perhaps the most striking of which is the emphasis placed upon practical work. Thus the BFI's recommendations for the 'Performance' strand of *Media Technologies* at Level 5 requires pupils to:

Be able to undertake simple assembly editing of sound tape, film or video; be able to log material taped or filmed, and plan a final edit.
(Bazalgette, 1989)

In similar vein, the Arts Council's 'End of Key Stage Statements' for Key Stage 3 include the suggestion that pupils should be able to 'Contribute to the management and technical operation of a performance' (Arts Council, 1992). Equally interesting is the emphasis placed upon subject content. Pupils should be able to 'Recognise and describe some historical changes in media' (Bazalgette, 1989), for example, or 'Demonstrate a knowledge of drama from different times and places' (Arts Council, 1992). Even in areas where English teachers might expect to find themselves on safe ground, unexpected challenges arise. Thus, the 'Performance' strand for Media Languages at Level 3 includes the recommendation that pupils should be able to:

Recognise *as conventions* certain features of media forms and genres (e.g. who speaks direct to camera and who does not; how invisible 'effects' such as speed, impact etc. are shown in comic strips).

(Bazalgette, 1989)

And while the Arts Council End of Key Stage Statement for Key Stage 3 includes, under 'Responding', the familiar English injunction to 'Reflect upon and evaluate the plays they see or in which they take part, justifying preferences', the exemplar material gives it a clear drama bias:

After a theatre visit, discuss the effectiveness of some of the design elements used in the production.

(Arts Council, 1992)

Finally, both documents make it unequivocally clear that English is by no means the only subject which has close connections with drama and media education. How many English teachers would consider themselves qualified to teach pupils to:

Understand principles of:

- persistence of vision
  (e.g. flick books, zoetropes)
- magnification and projection
- mirror reflections and printing
- positive and negative images

(Bazalgette, 1989)

Or, in drama, to 'Use a variety of technical effects' which, according to the exemplar material, might include creating costumes and masks or 'working on the lighting' (Arts Council, 1992)?

The challenge facing teachers of National Curriculum English is to find ways of using drama and media work to promote the principles declared by Professor Cox's Working Group while at the same time helping their pupils to appreciate the integrity and independence of both subjects. The following descriptions of two separate schemes of work for Key Stage 3 pupils engaged in drama and media education offer suggestions as to how these apparently conflicting claims can be reconciled.

## USING DRAMA TO SUPPORT TEXTUAL STUDY

A mixed-ability class of Year 9 pupils are about to read the poem 'Mariana' in compliance with the 1995 Order's requirement that Alfred Lord Tennyson might be one of the poets studied during Key Stages 3 and 4.[5]

The instructions given to pupils might read like this:

## 1 EXPLORING THE LANGUAGE AND STRUCTURE OF THE POEM

- Divide into four groups. Each group is given one particularly evocative line from the poem to think about, for example, *In sleep she
  seemed to walk forlorn.* Learn your group's line by heart and then practise a choral recital of it experimenting with different styles: whispering,
  shouting, laughing, etc. Try splitting the group to vary the effect –
  echo, crescendo, diminuendo, for example.
- Create a tableau which expresses the meaning of the line for you. The
  other pupils are invited to look at the tableau and say what it means to
  them. Speaking in role as the character you are playing in the tableau,
  state in one sentence the thought that is uppermost in your mind at this
  moment. Compare your (and your character's) thoughts about the
  tableau with those of the audience.
- Working on your own, take a numbered envelope. Each envelope
  contains a different verse from the poem. Read your verse to yourself
  till it begins to make sense to you. Experiment with different ways of
  saying the lines.
- Find someone who is working with a verse different from yours. Ask
  them to close their eyes. Lead them by the fingertips around the room
  while you recite your verse to them. Choose a style of delivery: telling
  a humorous story; pleading; breaking bad news; complaining. Change
  places and repeat. Use the opportunity provided by being led through
  the darkness to help you focus your thoughts exclusively on the words
  you are hearing – the speaker of the lines is, literally and metaphoric-
  ally, your 'guide'.
- Pair up with other people who had the same verse to work on as you
  did. Splitting the lines between you in any way you wish, plan a telling
  of your verse in narrative form. Try to add the ingredients of suspense,
  contrast, variety of tone, sense of pace, climax. Will your tale end on a
  'cliff-hanger'? Tell your story in the style of a particular genre: for
  example, a horror story; a fairy-tale; a thriller; a romance. Will your
  telling obey the conventions of the genre or subvert them?
- Sitting together in a circle, the whole group tells the story of 'Mariana'.

## 2 ENTERING THE WORLD OF THE POEM

- Consider the people mentioned by Tennyson in the poem: there is
  Mariana herself, obviously; but who is the 'he' who 'cometh not'? And
  whose are the 'old faces', the 'old footsteps' and the 'old voices'? Who
  might the narrator be?
- Study Sir John Millais' picture of Mariana painted in 1851. Compare it
  with that of another Victorian artist, James Bell. What are the simi-
  larities or differences in the ways these two male artists have painted

Mariana? How do their portrayals of the poem accord with/differ from yours? What insights into the character and condition of Mariana do the paintings give you? Is there any significance in the fact that the poem and the paintings are all created by men?

• Using the help of history and art teachers and the school librarian, look for contemporary pictures or photographs which seem to you to represent most closely your impression of the other people mentioned in the poem. Are they young or old? Rich or poor? Male or female? Happy or unhappy? What might their relationship to Mariana be?

• Make a display of the pictures and photographs. Walk around the 'exhibition' and look at the pictures. Discuss them with other people. Which interest you most?

• Choose a character from one of the pictures. Give them a name, age, occupation and status. Study the clothes they are wearing, the expression on their face, their 'body-language'. Think about their past history. They are to represent the people mentioned in the poem. Why and how are they involved?

• Assemble for a group 'photograph'. Close your eyes. Listen to the teacher talk you back in time to 1830 (the year 'Mariana' was first published). What was it like to be alive in England then? (Think back to the research you did for your picture.) When you open your eyes, it will be 1830. On the command 'Freeze!' open your eyes and strike the pose assumed by the character you have selected. Hold the pose while the teacher reads a verse from the poem.

• Still in role, sit down in a circle with the rest of the group. In turn, the teacher will 'hot-seat' you about your character, status and motivation. You may disclose as much or as little about yourself as you feel appropriate. You must, however, listen carefully to what other people say (or choose not to say) about themselves and take these comments into account when framing your own story.

## 3  CREATING MEANINGS

• Get into small groups. Ideally, these should consist of seven pupils (one for each of the verses) so that by pooling your resources you can establish a sense of the whole poem. Each person has a copy of 'Mariana'. In turn, guide the rest of the group through your verse. Make a list of the questions about the poem which you feel need to be answered.

• Bearing your discussions in mind, reassemble as a whole group. It is the first day back at school after the summer holidays. Tell your friends your news and catch up on the latest gossip. When the teacher calls 'Change!' switch immediately into your 'Mariana' character. How does this change of character affect your relationships with the other people in the room? How does your character's status compare with theirs?

Move around the group until you find other characters of the same status as yours. Out of role, share your thoughts about the ways in which issues of class and gender might have influenced the relationships between people in Tennyson's day. What insights into the character and situation of Mariana does this give you?

- Find four or five other people who chose a character different in status from your own. Study the poem together and plan a prepared improvisation which answers the following questions: 'Who is Mariana?' 'Who is the 'he' mentioned in the poem?' 'Why is Mariana so miserable?' Alternatively, decide what it is about the text which puzzles you and use the improvisation to provide your own answers.
- Watch and discuss the improvisations. Which of the possible interpretations might the whole group be interested in developing together? Would it be possible to merge two or more storylines?
- Having agreed upon a focus for their work, the whole group (including the teacher) attempts to create a spontaneous improvisation which might bring the story to a close. Working in role again, the pupils assemble at the 'moated grange'. The teacher chooses a role (authority figure? relative? servant? messenger?) and enters the drama with the question, 'What has happened to Mariana?' The improvisation could be played straight through till an answer is found, or it would be possible to come out of role at significant points in the story to reflect upon what has taken place and to consider further developments.

## 4 PRESENTING TO AN AUDIENCE

- The whole class presents a choral reading of the poem. Different groups could take on the role of narrator, chorus, Mariana herself – or present alternate lines, sections or verses.
- Working in groups, the pupils choose five lines or phrases from the poem which they feel to be particularly evocative. Using only those lines as often or in whatever order they wish, they present a response to the poem.
- A narrator recites the poem while others present a mimed response to it. The players could wear make-up or costumes and masks and might, for example, present the piece in the style of a particular theatre form such as Greek tragedy or Noh theatre.

All of these responses could be scored for music and could make use of lighting, props and sound effects.

The activities described in this drama-based scheme of work provide numerous opportunities for language development across all three Profile Components of National Curriculum English. The contexts for speaking and listening, for example, are rich and varied, ranging from spontaneous, informal small-group discussion to the formalities of carefully rehearsed choral speech. Above all, pupils have the chance to work with a variety of audiences and to experiment with language registers not normally encountered either in the classroom or in the course of their daily lives.

Each of the drama activities presents imaginative opportunities for writing. Pupils could, for example, compose the journals, letters and accounts of the participants in the role play. This could be done as a reflective piece of work after the drama has finished. Alternatively, the writing could be produced 'in the heat of the moment' – in role as the action unfolds – so that the receipt of a letter from 'Mariana' delivered, say, just as the meeting at the 'moated grange' is about to begin, might directly influence the course of the subsequent improvisation. Nor need the writing be a solitary activity. Pupils working in role as the 'old faces' in the poem might compose together an account of their relationship with Mariana. Each member of the group might be asked to contribute only one word, phrase, sentence or paragraph at a time, so that the resulting piece of writing is truly communal. If more conventional 'literary critical' work is required, the pupils' sense of engagement will be all the more intense because they have 'lived' the poem 'from the inside' – by transposing it into another genre; by narrating it to other pupils; by asking questions of the text and offering answers to those questions in dramatic form; by studying its rhythms, sounds and vocabulary in order to create a choral reading; and, above all, by entering the imaginative world of the poem and working with the poet on the creation of new meanings.

This insight into the ways in which reader and writer meet in the text to create meanings is one of the most important contributions which drama can make to pupils' understanding of the reading process. There can be few more graphic ways of demonstrating the fact that poems are open to a multiplicity of readings and interpretations than to invite readers to take part in the activities outlined in the scheme of work above. To transpose Tennyson's poem into a fairy-story or a radio play; to shift the focus from Mariana herself to one of the poem's peripheral characters; to construct the drama around the things the poem does not mention rather than those it does – all these strategies raise important questions about structure and convention, plurality of meaning, the relationship between reader and author.

## AN EXAMPLE OF MEDIA STUDY SUPPORTING AN APPROACH TO SHAKESPEARE

The scheme of work for media education is designed for the same year group as that of the drama. It focuses, again, on the *Selection of Literature* section of the 1995 Curriculum and is inspired by the suggestion that pupils should be:

> encouraged to appreciate the distinctive qualities (of works written in previous centuries) through activities that emphasise the interest and pleasure of reading them rather than necessitating a detailed, line-by-line study.
>
> (SCAA, 1994)

Following the spirit of the suggestion, this project aims to do more than simply teach the pupils how to parrot answers to reductive SAT comprehension questions. Instead, they are invited to consider how 'Shakespeare' can be created, mediated and received as an ideological construct in contemporary British society.

The instructions might read like this:

- Collect as much material relating to Shakespeare as you can find. This can include examination questions, editions of the plays and sonnets, books and critical articles on his work; but you should also look out for less conventional, 'academic' references in newspapers, magazines, adverts, cartoons, stationery, travel brochures, badges, theatre and film posters, commemorative mugs, etc.
- Think about the ways in which Shakespeare is portrayed. Do any patterns emerge? If you knew nothing at all about the man, what impression of him and of his status in contemporary society would you gain from studying this material?
- Focus upon the language, particularly that used by critics and GCSE and SAT examiners when writing about Shakespeare. In what ways are we allowed/not allowed to talk and write about him?
- Review two arts programmes – one from television and one from radio. At what time and on what channel/station are they broadcast? How are they advertised in the broadcasting schedules? What kind of audience are they trying to reach? How are they organised and presented? What kinds of language do they use? In what ways do the conventions of the two media differ from each other? Do you find the programmes interesting? Would anything be lost if they were taken off the air?
- Script and then record a five-minute feature on the Shakespeare play you are studying. You should imagine that it will be broadcast on one of the arts programmes you have reviewed. Who do you think will/ will not be listening/watching? What would the audience want to know about the play? How will you present the information? What kinds of language and what accents will the presenters use? Suppose the programme is broadcast on an independent station; what kinds of advertising might you expect to see before, after and during the commercial break?

- Devise a market research questionnaire on your feature and distribute it to the rest of the class for completion after the 'programme' has been 'broadcast'. If you were buying advertising space on the arts programme, what kind of information would you want to elicit from the questionnaire? Would the contents of the questionnaire be different if you were either the director of the programme or the person responsible for the arts output of the station as a whole?
- Analyse the results of the questionnaire and present a report to the station controller.
- In pairs, prepare an improvised response to the feature. You are listening to/watching the broadcast together. One of you is interested, the other is not. What are your motives? What is your status in relation to the broadcast (are you intimidated/bored/inspired by it, for example)? Enact your improvisation as the broadcast is played. Try to respond, not only to what it says, but to the way the material is presented. If possible, the improvisations should be recorded. Out of role, compare the characters' responses with your own. As a whole class, consider the issues which emerge.
- Interview Year 10 or 11 GCSE Literature pupils about their attitudes towards and experience of studying Shakespeare. Compare their views with your own and with those of adults – teachers and other school staff, perhaps, or relatives and friends. (Was it really better in 'the good old days'?) Record the responses. What kind of picture emerges?
- Drawing upon all the recorded material you have assembled during the project, create a response to Shakespeare in a medium of your choice – collage, photographs, audio tape, video, etc. If it is not logistically possible to compile an actual audio or video tape recording, prepare a transcript or a storyboard as an alternative.

As with the drama scheme of work, so here the pupils are offered a range of contexts, purposes and audiences for informal and formal speaking and listening and writing activities. An extra dimension is added in that issues of accent and dialect, language and power – implicit in the 'Mariana' project – are brought to the fore when the pupils are invited to think about the modes of discourse through which 'high culture' is mediated on radio and television. Particularly interesting is the way in which this work allows pupils the opportunity to experiment with forms of writing (interviews, reports, questionnaires, reviews, transcripts) which depart from those well-worn school alternatives of story and critical essay.

Most important of all, this scheme of work issues a radical challenge to the theories of mediation and reception represented by the 'cultural transmission' model of English which were enshrined in the 1993 Key Stage 3 Anthology and the revised Order. The authors of those documents require pupils to read *Rasselas* or *Romeo and Juliet*, for example, because they as experts have decided that those particular texts will do the children good. The media project on Shakespeare, on the other hand, encourages pupils to question that authority by asking, 'Why and how do you want me to read this?' 'How was this text produced?' 'Who has ownership of it and how do they wish to use that power?'

## MEETING SOME OF THE CHALLENGES

If English teachers approve of the kinds of activities and ways of working outlined here and wish to remain true to the Cox Working Party's pledge to keep drama and media education alive in their classrooms, they must meet a number of important challenges. The first is the need to treat the English Order – in whatever form it eventually takes – as an enabling rather than a restricting document. Both the schemes of work described in this chapter have been based, deliberately, upon one of the most controversial statements in the current Order: the requirement for all children to study pre-twentieth-century literature and the works of Shakespeare. Both schemes of work could be mapped against the proposed Programmes of Study and level descriptions with enough rigour to satisfy the most thorough OFSTED Inspector. Even with the emphasis on 'major works of literature from the English[6] literary heritage' and the primacy of 'Standard English', they will still offer many exciting opportunities for work in drama and media education.

The problem is, these opportunities are largely implicit rather than explicit – a series of hints to those 'in the know' rather than clear guidance for the uncertain. Take two examples from the new proposals for AT1. The *Key Skills* section of the Programme of Study for Key Stages 3 and 4 states that pupils should be taught to 'negotiate consensus'. Is that not something which drama teachers and their pupils work at every day, whether establishing the role-play 'contract', rehearsing a presentation or plotting a lighting plan? In the same place, the proposals also state that pupils should prove themselves able to 'modify their ideas in the light of what others say'. Could that instruction not be read as an opportunity to explore the concept of *Media Agencies* – by studying the processes by which a novel, for example, develops from first draft to publication?

Media education deserves particular consideration in this context. The Draft Proposals appear to give it scant attention; yet they are in fact full of coded references to the subject. There is the requirement that pupils develop 'the ability to adapt forms and genres for specific purposes and effects'; or write 'advertisements, newspaper articles . . . screenplays'; or 'reflect upon the use of language in a variety of media'. Most important of all, the fundamental principle that 'radio and television' can be regarded as 'non-literary and non-fiction texts' (SCAA, 1994) is conceded in the

*Selection of Literature* section for Key Stages 3 and 4. It was typical of the equivocal nature of the Draft Proposals' approach to media education that this crucial point should be made in such a furtive manner – almost as though the subject were being smuggled into the National Curriculum.

This suggestion that English teachers should approach the new English Order positively and with imagination does not mean they should give it an unequivocal welcome – as the critique in the earlier part of this chapter demonstrates. There are elements which should be treated with great caution by teachers committed to drama and media education. In his introduction to the 1993 precursor of the current document, the Secretary of State made it clear that the *adult needs, cross-curricular* and *cultural heritage* models of English were to be given priority over *personal growth* and *cultural analysis* under the new dispensation:

> English is at the heart of the National Curriculum. . . . All other learn-ing depends crucially upon the mastery of the fundamental skills of the English language, which are vital not only for educational and cultural development but also for our economic growth and competitiveness . . . . The sooner children master the basic skills and become confident users of Standard English, the sooner they can benefit from the other subjects taught in the curriculum, and the sooner too they can start to explore more advanced language skills and enjoy the pleasures and rewards of our [sic] literature.
>
> (DFE, 1993)

By suggesting that the *cultural heritage* and *adult needs* models of English are more important than the others, the new proposals privilege content over process. Teachers must teach, and pupils must learn. Such auth-oritarian transmission models of teaching do not suit drama or media education:

> Children are not seen as passive recipients but as active meaning-makers who have already made considerable learning progress in their immediate environment before they ever come into the classroom.
>
> (Neelands, 1984)

In the case of drama, the experience which children bring with them into the classroom is of pretending and imagining through play, of making relationships, of knowing what it is to be alive. In the case of media education, it consists of the 'extensive existing knowledge of media categories and media language' (Goodwyn, 1992) absorbed by every pre-school child who has ever watched television, listened to the radio or looked at a comic. The second challenge, therefore, is not to let the Order impose reductive models of practice in the English classroom or en-courage low expectations of the pupils.

It is likely, too, that teachers sympathetic to drama and media education will feel uneasy about John Patten's use of such definitions as 'suitable literature' and 'texts of central importance to our literary heritage' (DFE, 1993) even in the watered-down form of the 1995 Order. If some texts are centrally important, others must be less so. Likewise, *our* literary heritage must be different from *their* literary heritage (whoever 'they' may be). Media teachers do not categorise texts in this hierarchical way. Describing the influence which Michael Halliday's work on language exerted on the English curriculum of the 1960s and 1970s, Andrew Goodwyn observes:

> Halliday's work is concerned with language as a meaning making system and so all texts can be approached as significant. Potentially this places the study of an advertisement alongside that of a poem or the study of a speech from Shakespeare alongside that of a present-day politician.
>
> (Goodwyn, 1992)

David Buckingham has argued that the hierarchical approach to texts advocated by John Patten can already be found in the media references to the 1990 English Order which, he suggests, privilege 'non-fictional media' at the expense of 'the fictional media that children watch, read and enjoy'. Were teachers to adopt this approach, it would be difficult for them to resist the temptation of using media education as a way of asserting their own cultural values and belittling those of their pupils. Buckingham warns:

> It is difficult to avoid simply setting oneself up as a higher authority, in contrast to the lies and distortions of the media; or to end up implicitly demonstrating the superiority of the so-called 'quality' press to the tabloids one's students or their families actually read.

And he asks:

> Is the aim of media education simply to produce 'informed consumers' of *Newsnight* or *The Sunday Times*, or to obtain consent to the teacher's preferred interpretation of political events?
>
> (Buckingham, 1990c)

The Draft Proposals threatened to realise Buckingham's worst fears, not only because they were virtually devoid of explicit references to media education or because they did nothing to encourage the study of the fictional media texts which play such an important part in the lives of young people. Negative though these developments were, the Draft Proposals went even further by undermining the principle – enshrined in the 1990 English Order – that pupils should learn how to be creative users as well as critics of the media. Most of the references in the Draft Proposals were concerned with the reception rather than the construction of media texts. Consider – to take just one example – this statement from the *Key Skills* section of Attainment Target 2, Key Stages 3 and 4:

Pupils should be given opportunities to read non-fiction and non-literary texts in order to:

- select information;
- compare and synthesise information drawn from different sources;
- make effective use of information in their own work;
- evaluate how information is presented.

(SCAA, 1994)

There is no suggestion that pupils might also read such texts in order to learn how to make their own.

The issues of textual hierarchy at Key Stages 3 and 4 face English teachers starkly in the provisions for drama, where the exemplars for pupils' reading are limited (on no clear principle) to Marlowe, Priestley, Shaw and Sheridan. As for fiction and poetry, all the authors in the pre-1900 lists come from the Anglo-American tradition. There are only six women in the fiction section and three among the poets. Few 'New Commonwealth' writers are to be found in any of the post-1900 sections. And as for works in translation . . .

Ask most English teachers what drew them to teaching in the first place and their answers will probably include something about the desire to share their love of literature with young people and to alert them to the machinations of politicians, advertisers and the power of the popular media. There is a danger that the revised Order's reassertion of the distinctions between 'high' and 'popular' culture might have a seductive appeal. The third challenge, then, is to recognise that a commitment to drama and media education in English implies a commitment to a particular kind of teaching. It means working and learning alongside pupils rather than lecturing them from the blackboard. It means recognising that 'texts include not only books' (NCC, 1990) and that the phrase 'our literature' has a global rather than a narrowly nationalistic application. It means valuing the languages, cultures and learning which pupils bring with them to school, rather than attempting to impose some kind of cultural hegemony upon them.

The fourth challenge facing English teachers is the need to recognise that drama and media studies are subjects in their own right. Both the schemes of work described in this chapter require a degree of specialist knowledge and both provide opportunities for explorations which take pupil and teacher away from the familiar territory of English. The 'Mariana' project assumes an understanding of drama modes and 'theatre forms'. The section entitled 'Presenting to an audience' requires some knowledge of the theatrical conventions and traditions used by different cultures from around the world and an ability to work with masks, mime, costume, make-up, lighting, sound. Similarly, the media project on Shakespeare addresses the six Areas of Knowledge and Understanding described by the BFI. If the pupils are to derive maximum benefit from it, they must understand what terms like *Media Agencies* or *Media Representations* mean. On a practical level, they need to be able to use a camera or tape recorder or microphone. They need a working knowledge of media languages.

The challenge here is to make sure that, somehow, pupils are given access to this subject knowledge. The ideal solution would be for English departments to argue the case for the provision of drama and media specialists who could establish a comprehensive and coherent curriculum programme across the key stages in both subject areas. Teachers of English (and other subjects) could then draw upon this resource as the need arose, confident that their pupils would be familiar with, say, the terms of the role-play contract or the meaning of the phrase 'media agencies'. In the world of local management of schools, academic league tables and financial constraint, this solution is looking increasingly utopian. A more realistic approach would require the members of the English department to share responsibility for the acquisition of the relevant knowledge and skills between them – or, even better, to realise that colleagues in other subject disciplines might have help to give and claims to make upon drama and media education. What have art teachers, for example, to say about mask work or media categories? How might a science teacher contribute to a lighting plot or the study of media technologies?

Drama and media education can provide powerful contexts for the development of language, creativity and imagination. They can help us to know ourselves and other people better and to understand how we are positioned in and by our culture. They can help us to celebrate cultures different from our own. For all these reasons, the relationship between English, drama and media education is under threat. And for all these reasons, we must do everything in our power to preserve, strengthen and develop it.

## NOTES

1. I intend to follow Professor Cox's Working Group by reserving the term 'media studies' for specialist study and using 'media education' more generally, to refer to pupils' analysis and production of media artefacts.
2. Department of Education and Science/Welsh Office, (1989) *National Curriculum: From Policy to Practice*, HMSO, London, para 3.8
3. For accounts of the way in which the relationship between English and drama and English and media education developed, see respectively D Hornbrook (1989) *Education and Dramatic Art*, Blackwell Educational, Oxford, and L Masterman (1992) *Teaching the Media*, Routledge, London

4. It is often forgotten that the Working Group was actually asked to consider the place of drama and media education within National Curriculum English as part of its remit.
5. 'Mariana' was first published in 1830.
6. For an excellent discussion of the notion of 'Englishness' in literature, see B Naidoo (1994) 'The territory of literature: defining the coastline', *English in Education*, Spring, Vol. 28, No. 1, pp. 39–44.

## REFERENCES AND FURTHER READING

Abbs, P (1982) *English Within the Arts*, Hodder and Stoughton, London
Arts Council (1992) *Education: Drama in Schools*, Arts Council
Arts in Schools Project (1990) *The Arts 5-16: A Curriculum Framework*, Oliver and Boyd, Edinburgh
Barthes, R (1977) *Image, Music, Text* (translated by Stephen Heath), Fontana, London
Bazalgette, C (ed) (1989) *Primary Media Education: A Curriculum Statement*, British Film Institute
Bowker, J (ed) (1989) *Secondary Media Education: A Curriculum Statement*, British Film Institute
Buckingham, D (ed) (1990a) *Watching Media Learning*, The Falmer Press, Brighton
Buckingham, D (1990b) 'English and media studies – making the difference', *The English Magazine*, No. 23, Summer
Buckingham, D (1990c) 'English and media studies – getting together', *The English Magazine*, No. 24, Autumn
Cox, B (1991) *Cox on Cox: An English Curriculum for the 1990's*, Hodder and Stoughton, London
Crinson, J and Leak, L (eds) (1993) *Move Back the Desks: Using Drama to Develop English and Cross-Curricular Themes*, NATE
DES (1989a) *National Curriculum: From Policy to Practice*, HMSO
DES (1989b) *English for Ages 5 to 16*, HMSO
DES (1989c) *Drama from 5 to 16: Curriculum Matters 17*, HMSO
DES (1990a) *English in the National Curriculum* (No. 2), HMSO
DES (1990b) *Aspects of Primary Education: The Teaching and Learning of Drama*, HMSO
DFE (1993) *English for Ages 5 to 16*, HMSO
DFE (1995) *English in the National Curriculum*, HMSO
Eccles, D (1989) *English Through Drama*, Hutchinson, London
Goodwyn, A (1992) *English Teaching and Media Education*, Open University Press, Milton Keynes
Hornbrook, D (1989) *Education and Dramatic Art*, Blackwell Educational, Oxford
Jeffcoate, R (1992) *Starting English Teaching*, Routledge, London
Masterman, L (1982) 'Television and the English teacher', in Adams, A (ed) *New Directions in English Teaching*, The Falmer Press, Brighton
Masterman, L (1992) *Teaching the Media*, Routledge, London
McGregor, L et al. (1977) *Learning Through Drama*, Heinemann Educational Books, Oxford
*Media Education*, (1991) Hodder and Stoughton, London
NCC (1989) *National Curriculum Council Consultation Report: English*, NCC, York
NCC (1990) *English Non-Statutory Guidance*, NCC, York
NCC (1992) *National Curriculum English: The Case for Revising the Order*, NCC, York

NCC (1993) *The National Curriculum and its Assessment*, (Interim Report), NCC, York

Neelands, J (1984) *Making Sense of Drama: A Guide to Classroom Practice*, Heinemann Educational Books, Oxford

Neelands, J (ed) (1992) *Learning Through Imagined Experience*, Hodder and Stoughton, London

Neelands, J (ed) (1993) *Drama and IT: Discovering the Human Dimension*, NCET/NATE

SCAA (1994) *English in the National Curriculum: Draft Proposals (May 1994)*, School Curriculum & Assessment Authority

# Chapter 11

# Key Stage 4

## Back to the future?

*Nick Peim*

---

## THE STATE OF ENGLISH

The loss of 100 per cent coursework assessment in English at KS4 has meant a very significant shift in the practices of English teachers: 100 per cent coursework assessment schemes had become the norm in English teaching. One exam board, for example, reports that for English Literature alone they now have something in the region of 85,000 candidates for external assessment, now dominated by timed examinations, whereas previously they had something in the region of 5,000. Schemes of work, now much more an explicit requirement, have been adjusted to meet the needs of the newly defined set of parameters. With both English and English Literature, the new form of examination has been very much more clear about what the subject should assess, about what the subject effectively consists of. The identity of English, problematic throughout its history, had never been clearer.

The Dearing Report, in response to the outlined structure for KS4, has done little to change the fundamental reassertion of the central features of English. It has perhaps helped to soften the transition, from the very much more freely defined 100 per cent coursework schemes, which might have included all sorts of things, officially and unofficially. The Dearing Report, though, still refers to 'the correct use of standard English' without embarrassment; in the Dearing Report English Literature is still defined by exemplary texts – without addressing any questions about how texts get to be – or not to be – exemplary. Included, for instance, at KS3/4 in 1994 were Leslie Norris's poetry, the writings of Stan Barstow and Berlie Doherty as well as the non-fiction of Winston Churchill. Literature is laid out for you, along with the more familiar names and texts – so familiar perhaps that we no longer think even to question why they are there, let alone what we do with them and why we do it. Not that I am complaining about any of these particular inclusions, nor do I have anything against any of the above-mentioned writers or the texts associated with their names. It is how they became installed and then demoted from the range of exemplary texts that is of interest. How do they come to be English Literature? The process, if there is one, remains hidden and mysterious, perhaps decided on various committees or 'quangos', in accordance with the reading habits and predilections of a minority?

There can be little doubt that the effect of the recent changes in English at GCSE/KS4 has been very significant in terms of the detail of what gets taught, in terms specifically of limiting the range of texts taught at what is now KS4 in the name of English Literature and its public assessment and in the range of legitimate approaches to texts. It is likely to be universally conceded, whether for ill or for good, that the subject at this level in schools has become much more strictly defined and that the options open to teachers, and for students, have been much more strictly delimited. Although the assortment of texts that may be studied on any KS4 English Literature syllabus may hang together rather oddly, there is no doubt about what kind of thing they are, nor is there any doubt about what is an appropriate approach for this subject to take to the texts it deals with.

Tiering – another innovation of the new order – has serious implications, too, and represents a serious attack on one of the fundamental tenets of liberal English: that students are not predetermined as to their levels of attainment. The tiering of exam papers suggests strongly that results are in some broad sense at least predetermined and that whole groups of students are necessarily excluded from the higher levels of attainment, or suggests that whole groups of students will find certain texts or certain questions on texts beyond their reach, and that this unreachability may be predicted in advance. This is an uncomfortable position for a subject that has largely and publicly tended to find its relations with examining and assessment problematical, claiming to represent differences but being open to them at the same time. Tiering has been particularly problematic for the liberal vanguard (though may one not wonder that negative grading on an A–G scale – coursework or no coursework – never aroused the same degree of dissent?)

The teaching of English has changed in terms of quite specific writing skills that now need to be given new emphasis. Writing was being taught and assessed in coursework, but now it is clear that certain types of writing have to be taught. It is no longer possible to claim with such certainty that the writing done in English is good for the soul, or that it is a preparation for real writing in real life. Now it is at least partly a training in writing for the exam, and this applies also to other elements of the subject, including reading, but also including general meaning/sense making processes of interpretation. These have been significantly reduced to a training to perform certain readings in the reined-in context of the exam. In both English and English Literature the exam questions, and the kinds of response they have generated, have been lamentably predictable.

The choice of texts for KS4 literature examinations has had serious resourcing implications for departments struggling on limited budgets, but has also meant a shift in the approach to reading and textual analysis. The form of the literature exams tends to encourage the study of the single texts around which wider reading may be organised. But the approaches to the reading and interpretation of those texts, in so far as they are examinable, are more strictly delimited – explicitly, anyway – than with 100 per cent coursework schemes where it was theoretically possible, at least, for a vast range of texts to be addressed according to a range of approaches and principles.

English teachers may be left wondering how the new order can allow for the kind of good practices of English teaching that had become standard with 100 per cent coursework schemes. The hardening of the boundaries of English and English Literature is likely to have meant a restriction of practices; more significantly, though, it seems to me, the hardening of the boundaries of the subject has meant a crisis in terms of the identity and constitution of English, in ways that are revealing about the limitations, the inadequacies of the dominant models of English that went before. The traditional model has been found to be palpably restrictive and to fail even to fulfil its apparently utilitarian functions; the liberal model has been found to be less liberal, more compromised than before, if only by the ease with which it has slid into the present order of things.

## MAKING SENSE OF THE CRISIS: AN ALTERNATIVE MODEL

The coming of KS4 has powerful implications for the idea of the history of English as progress. In my view this myth of gradual and necessary progress has been compromised by the transition from previous models of an expansive, inclusive subject to a restrictive, strictly bounded set of practices. In spite of nominal protests by various bodies representing English teachers, the transition has been smoothly effected. This easy reversion itself seems to me to comment on the nature of changes and shifts in English that had been heralded, often by their own liberal instigators, as the road to liberation. How much, we may ask, had the professional identity of English teachers been disentangled from ideas centred around Standard English and Literature, for example? We may ask what the position was of those who were clamouring for more media studies to be included within English while they remained silent about the compromised category of literature, for example, a category that media studies itself would have difficulty entertaining as a textual body with special properties. These same advocates of an expansive English have also had little to say against the supremacy of Standard English as the model of excellence in 16+ assessment.

The critical reading I propose is informed by my own constructed version of 'critical theory', pieced together from materials that are and have been for a long time now freely available and that do have a significant place in other subject disciplines: an alternative set of ideas about language, texts and institutions. These ideas come from what has been loosely called post-structuralist theory, allied with well-established positions in the sociology of education and sociolinguistics and with developments in cultural theory.

This perspective effects a departure from the ideas that have, historically, dominated the subject, and have provided the terms for discussion and debate about its function, about what it is and about what it should be: ideas about texts, about language and institutions, specifically educational institutions, emerging from this perspective, are likely to undermine the established and taken for granted authority of the subject. In the realm of the humanities these post-structuralist discourses constitute something in the nature of a 'Copernican revolution'. While the position I attempt to describe here – drawn partly from this perspective – is highly critical of what English has been, it will propose that these radical theoretical developments may very positively provide the occasion for redefinition and reorientation of the institutional identity and practices of English. This position is critical of the traditionalist, back-to-basics account of the subject *and* is equally critical of more liberal accounts based on ideas such as creativity. In place of these notions, though, may be installed a range of productive ideas for dealing with language, texts and textuality.

## THE MYTH OF PROGRESS AND THE PROGRESSIVE MYTH

The recent history of English – with its series of governmental interventions, governmental control of the curriculum being made explicit – is sometimes represented as the triumph of the powers of darkness over the forces of enlightenment. English teaching – in the past aligned with progressive and liberal, liberationist ideals – now faces a dark age. Many teachers now experience their professional status as diminished in the light of what they describe as unwarranted government intervention in the details of the curriculum.

Precisely how far this gloomy view of the present state of English *is* entertained by English teachers across the nation is at the moment unknown, though. It may be that the majority of English teachers are unaffected by or indifferent to the loss of 100 per cent coursework schemes, for instance. There is, in fact, no readily available mechanism that might give us access to such knowledge. What we do know for sure is that the same body of teachers – represented as resentful of the new set of restrictions of the subject – is now actually teaching the new order. Whether this is being done with the same degree of commitment, energy, enthusiasm as ever, or whether it is being done in grudging bad faith, must also currently be largely unknown. This seems to raise the questions about how English teachers perceive their role. Do English teachers as a uniform body, subscribe generally perhaps to broadly agreed, even though implicit, principles? However you answer these questions a problem remains of how to speak for a disparate body, but one united in its continued practice of a scheme of work that some are claiming is against its better professional judgement and that contravenes its essential principles.

The uncertainty here about the nature of the English teaching body indicates clearly that the myth of the progressive history of English has been rudely interrupted. The National Curriculum, welcomed once, even by many liberals, as the final phase of the proper rationalisation of the properly progressive values of English, and their proper institutionalisation, has, it seems, turned against those who were once prepared to give it good entertainment. A government apparently unsympathetic to liberal ideals in English teaching has been intent on closing down options and restoring a rigidly limited version of language and literacy. Is the best future that can now be hoped for the nostalgic dream to restore what was?

I would argue, though, that any nostalgia for past schemes of English is misplaced. The recent series of government interventions in the details of curriculum does not seem to signal the fatal blow to the myth of the natural progress of the subject. The myth of English as enlightenment and as progressive in itself has always had to deny significant aspects of the subject: for example, that it has been content to endorse a limited range of texts that do not correspond to most people's cultural experiences, that it has continued to be involved in making negative judgements, via exam assessment systems, about people's languages. The demise of the myth of progressive English means that the subject's relation to government can no longer be hidden and that the subject must acknowledge its relations with powerful forces and institutions. It must face up to what it has been in spite of the liberal rhetoric of the subject.

The rhetoric of the natural, inevitable progress of English has ignored its more illiberal practices, including the institutional function of English to act as a kind of cultural filter in relation to issues of language and textuality. This rhetoric has been implicated in the continuation of a subject valorising a limited set of linguistic and textual competences and knowledge. Not only have the texts of English been notoriously limited in range. Reading and writing practices have been limited, too. Reading through character, for example, a cornerstone of both liberal practices and the new KS4, is a quite restricted and restricting reading practice. Personal response engages a very limited set of techniques for engaging with texts. And personal, imaginative writing, seen by some as the very heart of

English, represents only one, relatively narrow mode of dealing with the massively diverse field of writing.

The sociology of education – largely banished from discussions about English – may coldly remind us of some of the discriminatory functions of English in secondary education, in relation to grading and the chances for educational success. To claim that the loss of one form of examining this subject – which is likely to replicate identical processes of distinction – represents the loss of a significant component of secondary education at its most adventurous and far reaching – as has certainly been implied by many of the appointed spokespeople for English – is to fall simply for the progressive myth. Now English teaching may have to confront the impossibility of representing the subject as offering a uniquely progressive set of practices and ideals on the curriculum. This loss of innocence, though, need not necessarily be cause to mourn.

## REDEFINING ENGLISH IN SCHOOLS

Clear directions exist for a future of a subject encompassing language and text, like English, but unlike the present form of English. This subject would be differently constituted, taking on those broad categories in a far more theoretically explicit and aware manner, a subject recognising that there are (many, various) ideas about reading and writing, that different positions and approaches may be taken in relation to those apparently natural activities. This means deconstructing the favoured categories of English – like literature, like personal response, creativity, imaginative engagement, for example – to open up a realm of possibilities at present excluded by those favoured categories.

The present version of the National Curriculum with its particular form of KS4 assessment is indicative of the identity of the subject. The changes introduced by KS4 in 1992 have been quietly accepted. The relatively easy switch to KS4 assessment itself may serve to remind us how English has functioned – and what habits of thought have been steadfastly embedded in its continuation. It seems also indicative of some hard truths about professional identity: what it is that English teachers are contracted to do and to be. The switch from 100 per cent coursework GCSE to KS4 – with its terminal examinations, its set texts, its limited range of writing, all so apparently and radically different – has been effected, after all, with remarkable ease. The criteria of assessment have not changed that much. And the kinds of writing, the kinds of reading responses which will get rewarded, are highly likely to be all too predictably familiar. Maybe the scandal here is not so much the new forms of assessment, but that they will simply replicate the old forms, continue the same processes of discrimination on the same or all too similar grounds.

Although the end of the palmy days of 100 per cent coursework and the rewriting of the National Curriculum have been met with some public hair-tearing by English teachers, the changes they have wrought need not necessarily be the occasion for mourning. While KS4 could hardly be the occasion for unconfined joy on the part of committed English teachers, for English teachers wanting to explore new possibilities, interested in exploring the question of the constitution of a subject in the realms of language and textuality, theoretical reflection might be more useful than either dispirited resignation or cynical compliance. The theoretical awareness – afforded by a post-structural radical re-reading of language and textuality and all their massive implications for institutional practices – may point forwards to a new and different future for English, rather than looking back on the suspect glories of a mythic past.

## A SITE FOR CONTEST

One important and very positive consequence of the recent government interventions into the English curriculum could be to reconstitute the subject English as an arena for contest. Easy liberal confidence in progress – and the ensuing despair when that myth gets shattered – may be displaced by a more sharply critical awareness of issues, providing the impetus for a more theoretically charged and challenging view of the subject and its potentialities than we are used to hearing from either liberals or traditionalists. This latter position might signal the opportunity for a reconstruction of the professional identity of English teachers, actually enabling them to be active agents in the construction of the subject.

After all, some important points may be seen to emerge in recent public debates about English. It *has* been generally conceded that there are different versions of the subject; this has given rise to a more or less explicit kind of conflict about what English should be. Second, the subject is now clearly seen to be the bearer of important cultural significance; that the form of this significance might be contested has become widely acknowledged in the public arena. Third, governmental intervention, while illustrating, negatively, the political and intellectual disarray of the English teaching body, positively demonstrated that the constitution of the subject could be changed – one way or another – at a stroke by a critical and determined intervention.

## LITERARY EDUCATION AND LANGUAGE PRACTICES IN ENGLISH – THE LIBERAL/TRADITIONAL ALLIANCE

A brief vignette of a new realm of possibilities may be gleaned from examining some examples of textual reading practices in relation to the established idea of literature in English. Before making some sketchy suggestions about how this might be done, I would like to go over some of the arguments about the idea of literature in English in schools.

English and English Literature have been seen in close association. Some versions or accounts of the subject have held them to be necessarily intertwined – including KS4. Progressive English, while at times prepared to challenge some of the presumptions of canonical English Literature, has nevertheless always remained bonded to the idea of literature as a special and uniquely productive textual field. The uncertain status and being of the literary text – a primary object of English – raises in turn the problem of the identity of the subject. The identity of English has been to a significant extent founded on the idea of the literary text, and on the related idea of the value of a literary education.

One interestingly provocative thing about this, though, is that the literary text has changed its identity through the years. In effect, it is notoriously impossible to define what literature is – or what the limits of literature might be. Another interesting fact is that the contents and purposes of a literary education have been – historically, at least – equally unstable. Literature has been advocated in the name of traditional values, but also in the name of the more liberal idea of the exploration of individuals and their world. The function of literature, and the idea of literary education, has changed in accordance with changing discourses about learning, changes discourses within education. Literature has been remarkably accommodating in this sense. It has been prepared to change itself and to allow itself to be moulded by different sets of ideas and different cultural imperatives at different times. This protean quality may in one sense indicate an admirable flexibility. It indicates quite unequivocally, on the other hand, that any claims that may be made on behalf of literature to be or to represent anything specific must be abandoned.

The recent restoration of the set work at KS4 leaves English with the embarrassing necessity of specifying particular examples, where previously with GCSE it was possible to make vague gesturings in the direction of texts of literary merit, trusting that everyone knows what that means anyway. The texts proposed in 1994 for study at KS4 have no unifying identity and are never individually justified as objects of study: they appear without explanation or justification as *faits accomplis*. Looking at one syllabus on offer, texts for study at KS4 may be selected from a fairly bizarre range: *Great Expectations* by Charles Dickens, *A View from the Bridge* by Arthur Miller, *Sumitra's Story* by Rukshana Smith. 'The Individual And Society' option offers *The Friends* by Rosa Guy, *Roll of Thunder, Hear my Cry* by Mildred Taylor, *To Kill a Mockingbird* by Harper Lee. Add a touch of Shakespeare and a bit of pre-twentieth-century literature done for coursework (though why either should be compulsory is mysterious, surely) and you may have the grounds for attaining an official, state-registered qualification in English Literature.

There is not much canonical literature in the set text lists; the canonical and non-canonical consort together oddly here. What might be the parity between *Great Expectations* and *The Friends*? (What exactly *is* the literary merit of *The Friends*?) *Sumitra's Story* and *A View from the Bridge* make strange bedfellows. The inclusion of American literature, for example, may be read as a concession to significant trends. Is English Literature being redefined? How does this process occur? Who decides that *The Friends* is in, that it is comparable with *Great Expectations*, that *The Stud* or *Hollywood Wives* is out? Are the texts that are in chosen for their special merits, or are they chosen as especially illustrative of particular themes? Or are they chosen as especially relevant to the study of English Literature at this level?

From what perspectives, informed by what, other than certain, very limited reading techniques, is 'The Individual And Society' to be pursued? The criteria of assessment do not really offer very much to go on. There is no indication that theories of individuality, whether psychoanalytic theories of subjectivity or sociological material exploring the relations between the individual and society, or studies from a legal or historical perspective are to be favoured. The criteria of assessment put the emphasis rather on certain well-worn textual features, setting and character, for instance, rather than inviting a discussion about how texts might be seen to engage with these categories – the individual, society – from a number of different perspectives.

It seems clear that the notion of 'literary' education is questionable, where the literary refers to an uncertain but very limited body of texts. It follows that the idea of the set text in English is dubious. Why might we ask students to read *Great Expectations*? Because it is somehow worthy in itself? This is a philosophically very dubious notion. Because it reveals something about the time it is written in? Well, a minefield opens. In English justifications for literature are characteristically thin or non-existent. The value of literature – or what goes under the name of literature in English – is not argued for, questioned and is never the explicit focus of recommended modes of study.

The question, crucial though it may be – why do we require students to read and study *Great Expectations*? – has no clear answer. Answers that are offered – for example, that it is worthy of study in itself – are hollow. The point is, though, that *Great Expectations* is established and that simple fact of presence may be its use for an alternative, and deconstructive, practice of the subject.

The relation between literature – as a form of cultural experience signifying a certain kind of cultural identity – and other popular forms strikes immediately as a possible point of entry. This interface – still relevant as long as English claims the category of literature in the way it does as a special/distinct textual category to be valued in itself – may be usefully and extensively explored even under the new regime, perhaps more so when the category of literature is being promoted as an un-problematic category.

For many students literature represents an alien textual field. The way it is used means that it works as a kind of cultural filter sifting attitudes and responses – advocating some, encouraging others, dismissing these, excluding most and prohibiting still others. Literature represents the textual tastes of some but not of others, probably not most – and so many students stand disadvantaged culturally in the face of *Sumitra's Story* as much as in the face of *Great Expectations* or *Henry V*. Those, perhaps, who stand to gain from the education system's filtering processes are likely to feel much committed to it, or are likely to feel its intrinsic merit. Others may be positioned to experience their indifference to Literature as a lack, a personal or cultural deficit. For me it is the inadequacy of the category of literature that demands the production of new ways of dealing with texts. While literature remains in place in English the authority of the subject demands deconstruction, too.

## LITERARY EDUCATION: BREAKING THE MOULD

Questioning the centrality of literature, a practical programme offering a redefinition of reading practices might address the following points, might put them to use in particular teaching strategies and classroom practices:

- a phenomenology of reading: examining fundamental processes of reading; looking at what texts are, how they function; looking at the relations between texts and readers; (this may be one way of positively redefining what 'back to basics' might mean);
- definitions and categories of texts: how texts get categorised, different ways of categorising them, different institutions involved and their different constituencies: for example, popular culture, English Litera-ture, TV soaps, adverts, Shakespeare and newspaper articles on football;
- contexts of reading: institutions of reading, and their effects on reading practices and reading subjects; examining how people read and what forces determine the way they may read in different institutional contexts;
- conventional/alternative ideas about reading: looking at different con-ceptions of reading, how it works, what it is for, and so on; teaching explicitly that there are different theories about all this, that literacy is not one simply defined thing that all can aim for;
- ideas for textual analysis: for example, genre, codes, contexts, time, identities, gender, gaps, ideology; introducing alternative ideas and modes of analysis and understanding from the limited range con-ventionally proposed by English;

- ideology and interpellation: looking at how ideas about the world circulate in texts and discourses that position reading subjects – in many different contexts – differently; proposing ideas about how texts are caught up in social and political questions and issues; looking at how texts may influence individuals, how individuals may use texts – and what forces may be at work in all this;
- redefining the textual field: defining readers, within the educational context, in different ways; looking at how educational institutions have operated with very limited notions of literacy – and working to see how changes might be wrought in how schools, for example, teach *and* administer literacy competences.

The established use of the set text in English teaching is a far cry from all this. The reaffirmation of the set text, though, in KS4 signifies the impossibly limited scope of English – as well as its ideologically loaded nature. Contradictions and holes in the subject have simply been amplified by the recent government intervention re-establishing the set text, Shakespeare and pre-twentieth-century literature.

Deconstructively speaking, the set text may offer more the occasion for a new set of procedures for reading texts. This is likely to be far more inclusive of varied techniques for reading than the limited range of practices associated with English and clearly inscribed in the national criteria for formal assessment and in the attainment targets of KS4. Deconstructing English, though, is about more than finding new ways of reading or dealing with *Great Expectations*. About more than finding new games to play with *Henry V*, say, offering the same old outcomes. *Great Expectations* may be used, rather, to furnish the occasion for a deconstructive exploration of the very idea of textuality itself and – by examining how English has dealt with it, by looking at other possibilities – may actively challenge the existing authority of the subject.

## GREAT EXPECTATIONS

*Great Expectations* may provide as good an illustrative instance as any for an approach to textuality and textual issues. What follows suggests different approaches from those traditionally associated with ideas about textual authority (we read *Great Expectations* because it *is* great) or with those associated with personal response (we read *Great Expectations* to explore our own selves). Textual interrogation may be a more appropriate way of describing the approach offered here. It might be useful to con- sider *Great Expectations* as a starting point, if only because it is one of the exemplary texts of English.

*Great Expectations* may be questioned on a number of grounds. The identity of *Great Expectations* may furnish the occasion for a questioning of the traditional notion of an essentially significant or intrinsically valuable canonical literature. The idea of the universality of *Great Expectations* – and of the broader notion of literature loosely subscribed to by more recent, institutionalised (in exam syllabuses) ideas of English – may also be scrutinised. In the context of English Literature as an examined subject, critical theory may shift the ground of textual encounters: where the textual field is strictly under control, as in the case of KS4. Shifting the ground in this case means that *Great Expectations* cannot assume the stable, singular identity it may have done. Shifting the ground may also mean that reading techniques and practices that English does not embrace may come into play. In contrast to the limited scope of the reading practices of hitherto powerful models of English – the more liberal, avant-garde and traditional – the following textual issues may be addressed:

- The context of texts, the limits of texts and their meanings cannot be singular and assured: everything *Great Expectations* refers to must exist outside and beyond the text. Orlick, for example, is produced as a type, or stereotype: creative production actually selects from pre-existing ideas embedded in language.
- Textual identity and textual meanings are not self-producing. All texts relate to, are read against, other texts: *Great Expectations* cannot be understood in relation to itself alone; it has meaning only in so far as anything in it is recognisable as an example of a known textual form.
- Textual meanings are plural: there is no single reading of any text that can claim superior merit above any other; dominant readings may exist, but even these are likely to be incomplete, selective, and will often contradict themselves and one another. *Great Expectations* may be read as an indictment of social conditions in nineteenth-century England, or may be read as an example of the positive merits of nineteenth-century English culture.
- There are quite different ways of reading texts, and quite different perspectives: English deals with but one established mode of textual analysis, one that has been recently, systematically, challenged by a number of theories relating to textual fields, readers and reading instructions, for example.
- Texts belong to specific discourse which helps more or less to stabilise their potentially divergent, contradictory meanings.
- Discourses are related to social practices, and to specific institutional contexts. People are often organised differently in relation to these discourses and their texts, education being one powerful instance of such a practice or set of social practices within its own various, powerful institutions. *Great Expectations* 'belongs to' the discourse of literature; but it is shot through with innumerable other discourses, the discourse of personal identity, for example, and may be given a different inflection

if transposed into a different discursive arena – media studies, for instance.

This approach to the literary object does not entail a loss for students of access to knowledge they need for exams. This knowledge, though, may be framed and set against other knowledge. Deconstruction in this sense understands what it deconstructs – better than it understands itself: it deals with the very terms of the discourse it addresses. It enables consciousness of reading positions and affirms the constant interplay of culturally significant ideas in any reading event.

Here are examples of ways of interrogating the text which fulfil such a deconstructive approach:

| Proper names/agents/identities | Objects | Places |
|---|---|---|
| Pip | bread | the cemetery |
| Joe | brandy | the forge |
| Magwitch | file | the hulks |
| Miss Havisham | hammer | Little Britain |
| Orlick | anvil | Jagger's office |
| . . . | . . . | . . . |

Identify which of the above are *in and not in Great Expectations*, and which are only in *Great Expectations*.

For those that are both *in and not in Great Expectations*, what do they mean in *Great Expectations*, and not in *Great Expectations*?

What do we need to know about already in order to make sense of any of the above textual components?

What significance/function do they have in the text? Can any of them be given a single meaning or function?

What assumptions do we need to make about any of the above for them to operate within the narrative of *Great Expectations*?

What sort of gaps or questions are we left with in relation to any of the above?

Textual data: we may interrogate this endlessly: for example, what do we know about the hulks, the transportation system – how it worked (Magwitch's career, for example. Is it plausible?). Estella: what precisely do we know of Estella from the text? What information are we given, what clues, what certainties? But a more thoroughgoing critique of the claim that the text contains information to be interpreted may be undertaken.

Even if we take for our focus what we might assume to be in the text, its constituent element, as it were, the contexts are not quite so secure as the authors of the examination of English clearly assume. In what sense the character of Estella may be said to be within *Great Expectations*, then, can be seen to be a problematic question. Estella is not a 'character' in a fully embodied sense, any more than Orlick or Pip is – or President Kennedy or Eric Cantona, for that matter. Character is really just one, limited, way of reading certain textual clues and data. Estella is the product of a great deal of inference, embodied, in the main, by assumptions that any reading brings to the text. All sorts of cultural knowledge and assumptions about women, for example, all sorts of half-guesses must be made, all sorts of gaps must be left unfilled for Estella to 'function' in a coherent reading of the narrative of *Great Expectations*.

Estella is never fully present before us but must be read off from a gathering of textual clues. May we conclude that Estella is in *Great Expectations*? If Estella is a product of the imagination's interpretations of clues, it is perfectly possible to suggest then that Estella is merely the function of individual interpretation. And yet the clues given, linguistic clues, surely cannot be subject to the vagaries and differences of individual consciousness.

### The Intertextuality of Great Expectations

List texts that have a range of female characters in them: for example, TV soap opera and films.

List the different types of femininity and their different functions within the texts you've listed.

How would Estella fit into any of the texts you've mentioned? How might she be written into any of them? Sketch out some examples.

This kind of work may be developed in many ways. The point is to illustrate how our reading of Estella is constructed, not simply from the textual clues that *Great Expectations* offers, but also from our knowledge of other texts, and form our habitual ways of reading the signs they offer us.

## *GREAT EXPECTATIONS* TEXTUAL IDENTITY AND TEXTUAL STATUS

### Textual identity

Compare *Great Expectations* with the following texts:

*The Daily Mirror*
*Home and Away*
*Terminator 2*
A Madonna video

Sketch out some ideas for how *Great Expectations* might be transposed into other textual forms:

A Terminator film
*Home and Away*
A Madonna video

What would be the effects of these transpositions?

## Textual status

Consider the texts you compared with *Great Expectations* above.
   Is *Great Expectations* more complicated than any of them?

- Is it more relevant?
- Is it more interesting?
- Is it more full of useful knowledge?
- Is it more beneficial to study?

In what different circumstances might you make use of these different texts?
   Our understanding of texts depends to a large extent on our under-standing of many, perhaps innumerable, other texts. If this is true, then *Great Expectations* cannot be distinct from and uncontaminated by the order of text it is institutionally determined as being beyond or different from: narrative texts of popular culture. The general principle of inter-textuality raises the question of the identity of this text: where does it begin and end? What are its limits? How can meanings be fixed and determined?
   It also raises the further question of the identity of the text as a special kind of cultural object, possessing special value, questioning its being and place on the curriculum at all.

## DIFFERENT READING OF *GREAT EXPECTATIONS*

Is *Great Expectations* always the same

- wherever it is read?
- whoever reads it?
- whenever it is read?

Consider how changes in location, in the reader, in time might change *Great Expectations*. Give some instances of how changes in these might make *Great Expectations* different.

It may help to propose different locations, identities and times for the reading of *Great Expectations* to work out how readings may differ accord-ing to these variables. If it can be demonstrated that readings do differ – as they must, surely – according to them, then the idea of the stability of

*Great Expectations* as a signifying unity cannot be sustained. The idea of there being a single, stable or universal *Great Expectations* cannot be sustained. It is the case that no text can guarantee the conditions of its reading. We may then ask, 'Well, what *does* guarantee the conditions in which *Great Expectations* will be read?'

## TO SUMMARISE

One thing that remains certain about the new orders for English is that the reaffirmation of the central concerns of the subject is formulated on well-established lines. Literature remains defined as literary texts and the examination of language is constructed around the traditional categories of comprehension, letter writing and creative writing. All of these are based either explicitly or implicitly in the traditional practices of teachers and examiners. These are ideas adhering to such central assumptions of the subject as the notion that standard forms of response to texts are the response itself; or that 'grammar' and appropriate forms of writing can be defined as good or bad according to universally established criteria. The new orders are merely the old order.

The criteria of assessment in literature remain constructed around the familiar categories of character, particularly, plot and personal response. It is as though there were no other ways of reading literary or any other kind of texts. Criteria of assessment in English remain tied to categories like accuracy, sentence structure and vocabulary, as though these elements could themselves determine the quality of a piece of writing. Standard forms dominate as ever.

There is in all this much less space for the discourses that had appeared mainly on the established element of the periphery of English teaching, certainly in its more avant-garde quarters. Ideas and practices based on sociolinguistics, on media studies, on deconstruction, and even elements of the subject addressing political issues informed by an understanding of class differences, racial inequalities and gender bias have largely been excluded from the central definitions of English as a curriculum subject. They have been in effect banished from the core. That they were on the periphery, that they had not invaded the core of the subject, reflects the identity of English and the professional investments of those who operate within its bounds. Some English teachers implementing the new National Curriculum may be left with the uncomfortable sense that they are doing governmental work, presiding over domains they may have to recognise are ruled by powers beyond themselves. Those powers include the very discourses they have themselves lived by.

Post-structuralist redefinitions of language, discourse and cultural practices along with sociological and sociolinguistic critiques of schooling, and the lessons of recent public events in education, have both conspired to deconstruct the progressive model of the subject. Recent developments in cultural theory have rendered problematic the very idea of a stable and self-evident identity for English. English as we have known it, in its characteristic modes of organising ideas about language and about textuality, can only be described as an anachronistic institutional practice: not, in fact, as essentially progressive. The centrality of the idea of literature clearly illustrates this. The slipperiness of this apparently essential category has not prevented its remaining central to both traditionalist and liberal versions of the subject, those two 'poles' which may claim to represent different positions, but which have contested with one another merely to enable the continuation of a deeply anti-theoretical, and (therefore) ideologically conservative, subject.

English has been used as an element in the contest for certain ideas to dominate the field of mass education. The imposition of an apparently traditionalist and restricted model – as in current KS4 – may have the positive virtue of foregrounding the question about the proper domain and regime of the subject. This might positively be construed as a moment for redefinition, for the emergence of a consciousness, on the part of English teachers, of what they are about, of their relations with the various institutions within which their work is framed, of their relations to the politics of education, both in the immediate sense of intervention in the politics of change (via resistance of edicts, for example) and also in the sense of a wider political awareness of issues, including the politics of literacy, of language and textual matters. Such a redefinition of professional identity would be essential to the construction of a subject dealing with language and textuality that would be founded on theoretical awareness and that would be aware of its institutional functioning.

What has been explored here indicates, perhaps, how English, having failed to question its textual dealings, was open to the kind of reinstatement of set texts that we now see – with all the limitations of ideas and scope that implies. But it may also serve to show that this may not need to be the end of the story. Deconstructively speaking, the limits cannot be inscribed and alternative practices may flourish.

After all, it is the reading practices it is subjected to that determine the contents, identity, meaning and function of *Great Expectations* – or English.

## FURTHER READING

For an introduction to 'theory':

Richard Harland (1987) *Superstructuralism: The Philosophy of Post-Structuralism*, Methuen, London

Chris Weedon (1987) *Feminist Practice and Post-Structuralist Theory*, Basil Blackwell, Oxford

For an alternative view of language and language practices:

Fairclough, N (1989) *Language and Power*, Longman, Harlow
Trudgill, P (1974) *Sociolinguistics*, Penguin, Harmondsworth

For an alternative view of the functions of English in education:

Hunter, I (1988) *Culture and Government: The Emergence of Literary Education*, Macmillan, London

For classroom materials in the area of fiction:

Mellor, B, Patterson, A and O'Neill, M (1991) *Reading Fictions*, Chalkface Press, Australia (distributed through NATE, Sheffield)
(*Reading Non Fictions* is forthcoming.)

For a more full presentation of the above case with reference to classroom practices:

Peim, Nick (1993) *Critical Theory and the English Teacher*, Routledge, London

# Index